CW00427995

Lake Shore Drive

JOHN WILKINSON was born in London and grew up in Cornwall and Devon. He teaches at the University of Notre Dame, having worked in mental health services in the UK for three decades. He has published five previous volumes of poetry, including *Proud Flesh* (1986), *Flung Clear* (1994), and *Contrivances* (2003). A collection of criticism, *The Poetry of Excess*, is forthcoming from Salt in 2007.

Also by John Wilkinson:

Oort's Cloud (Barque)
Proud Flesh (Salt)
Flung Clear (Parataxis Editions)
Effigies Against the Light (Salt)
Contrivances (Salt)

Lake Shore Drive

JOHN WILKINSON

SALT

CAMBRIDGE

PUBLISHED BY SALT PUBLISHING
PO Box 937, Great Wilbraham, Cambridge PDO CB1 5JX United Kingdom

All rights reserved

© John Wilkinson, 2006

The right of John Wilkinson to be identified as the
author of this work has been asserted by him in accordance
with Section 77 of the Copyright, Designs and Patents Act 1988.

This book is in copyright. Subject to statutory exception
and to provisions of relevant collective licensing agreements,
no reproduction of any part may take place without the written
permission of Salt Publishing.

First published 2006

Printed and bound in the United Kingdom by Lightning Source

Typeset in Swift 9.5 / 13

This book is sold subject to the conditions that it shall not,
by way of trade or otherwise, be lent, re-sold, hired out,
or otherwise circulated without the publisher's prior consent
in any form of binding or cover other than that in which
it is published and without a similar condition including this
condition being imposed on the subsequent purchaser.

ISBN-13 978 1 84771 255 7 paperback
ISBN-10 1 84771 255 9 paperback

SP

1 3 5 7 9 8 6 4 2

for Maudie

Contents

Acknowledgments

Barque Press published *Iphigenia* as a pamphlet in 2004. The final part of this poem has been revised.

'Organise, Move and Back Up' was published as a broadsheet for a reading at the University of Maine on February 12, 2004.

Other poems have appeared in the print journals *Bad Press Serials*, *Chicago Review*, *Drill*, *The Gig*, *Poetry Review* and *QUID*, in the on-line journal *Free Verse*, and in the anthologies *100 Days* (Barque Press, 2001) and *River Pearls* (EPSI, Guangzhou 2005).

This book benefited from the generosity of North East London Strategic Health Authority in granting a sabbatical year which allowed the take-up of a Fulbright Scholarship at the Nathan S. Kline Institute for Psychiatric Research, New York. Many thanks to Carolyn Regan and Janet McMillan.

Lake Shore Drive

All hangs together, I am in chains. Unfortunately I do not quite
know what floor I am on, perhaps I am only on the mezzanine.

SAMUEL BECKETT

Just don't expect lemurs to magically appear from the fine print
of the self-storage contract.

KEVIN DAVIES

Mercator

A lovers' shadow, thumbed
from waxy & ambitious
skins advances to the knoll,
casts its bolt, sees eye to eye,

the sticking place is always
darling that reluctant
ever to seal over, coercive
pulls their troubled shade.

Merry co-star will deflect
as though impregnable,
spot spent position-taking
startles to the bigness there,

taps the shadowy mound
loosening caught heels.
Darling sweat the loud
thunder, let its rolls extend

crescendo on crescendo,
flattening a carefully-cut
circle. In San Diego, loaded
sequencers conceive cells.

Dateline

Fingers move across the buttons
in all-there, in nothing-doing,
am they being spoken to.
If you want help, go to the back wall,
in the one-person capsule
to the touch screen. Forensics
cleans up your footprint departed.

Alone they work in concert.
Without betraying a word, they work—
is that an improvised runway? Is
to the same end, is that blood?
that a gang-attack? It saw a severed
head below the elder bush,
or am I a report recently launched?

Save that for a one-man outburst:
there in the world, boulders of lint
shine, make clattering noises,
names are dropped, people dropped,
policies dropped, special effects
run the mill. Internal
motivation gallops in sealed units.

Abacus

A touch looped so to rest
constituted, which by maul
content, touched-on it
betrays. Geranium
traffic drips off the rain,

out of sight out of mind
steeply that it might linger.
Foxglove fingers
snuggling the figures
made for its drops to veer:

pray all activity heed
the one account, divining
bones, the turbid sky
slipping its distillate
from wire to wire, touch

paper, touchstone. What
was had by drip-feed,
run-off of the one
instalment, padding bones,
rolls in immaculate skin.

Squared Off

This is the same room, equable,
to itemize is not to have returned
stuffed with things ill-recollected
either upon this stele, or bellywise.

Are these the surroundings to love,
here were shaken down, frayed
or are they not let in? The things
leather, tarnished smiles, cold hands

scrabbling at valves but intermit,
bury vials during gaps in flow—
re-pump a negative pressure room.
Spins the stylus, floats the pointer,

taking stock of surroundings: are
things in their place, in balance—
favourite persons once counted out,
objects for distraint, sequestered?

A Reasonable Settlement

Here is how we shall settle down. Map
the neglected plot, build military roads
for the school run. Those poltergeists
can throw stones into the satellite nets—

Here is how we deal with obstructions.
Irrigate the soil with colourless blood,
worrying out stones. Poltergeists scuttle
to concoct their clumsy, abstract title-

deeds out of hardcore & galvanised &
corrugated, stretch-marked plastic sheets,
plotting some reality. Ghost mortgagers,
we shall make them real with a punch.

Cité Sportif

Cité Sportif: testing aerobically, by step change
sponsors the crisis so the constant will bricks burn.
Unilateral gives a hand blade-first to a domestic
falange hampered by no fingers follows through/
losing feet halted
lost half her face.
Spare this without fail
curated utmost measures clowning cutoff guns,
torn-blossom aesthetics, paper-eaters
                                        cannot obstruct
an armed proxy, artfully arrange their clippings.
   • Oxygen of suppression
   • Suck-out from the dug-in
   • The tell-tale account switch
wrist-flashing lane IDs
neon-clocked down the strip totally what stamped
intelligence docket couldn't, can you stomach, you
have no stomach which must be superscription
documents sent ahead, to add up to a fateful boy
dubbed incorrigible had from birth or by neglect
         traded for time in blocks,
         the flat soles cushioned,
         the Uzi clips were shucked—

options bud to bud maturing, evidence this moon-
face freewheels a urethral crook, heads for home,
made up, really made, what respect resections him:
His birth-repeat spatters
the real stomach contents not some installed shit.
   • Eat & cannibalise
   • Pastry-cut trainer soles

- Eat stadium *tropicália*
- This mental block

fly-posted, tag-painted to dissolve, dressed to cal-
culate aggressive daub, organize MP3s:
would an intelligence captain tremble at their well-
heeled, feasted song opening with bloody boxes
trodden down, stamped out?
    His own work. Solely. Stamps
authoritatively.
Native soil. Folds
plain enchiladas. Sunk ballads to regurgitate, for-
fend the fast food he'll have to chew then slew!
subversively, orbs crusted in portentous sugar,
seized scallops, interrogation suit has gold thread
detailing, monogram tweezered through each
    face-grating swabs
these legs, these hands, a man will round the bend
for first place on the last lap,
        mount the impregnable dais
A hard day
A Riefenstahl
fitness course
between holes could the bunker, could the green,
this hole draw back the skin like a parachute/
clingfilm-wrap what they spilt/ drove from earth
the fox & all proxies bearing parts in their mouths

I think not
I think not

Cité Sportif

Theatrical in their casting out, their eyes strew
engineer the woman they'd once conceived
adorns now bus shelters, nightclubs, wheel-
chairs with drawn-up hearts & carriage, hers
& others', match iconoclasts in rose-red cities,
holy place overlaid on holy place overlaid
where to go round the more scopes the whole.
    You are driving but across its range
    throwing up, throwing up.

Turn a corner down, turn down its dog-eared
corner, take the corner to see the velodrome
assemble all loose objects including humans—
in L'viv say, then copy, wire New Record Poll,
double crows-feet emblazoned on the sheets,
the critical targets trackside huddle, count,
tagged to every object twisting for aerial skier.
    Alive, the broidered initial
    but splints your bones' collision.

Using a proprietary measurement scheme,
what takes away wipes the grimace entirely,
nothing gives birth but count in time stitches
• Hold the torchlight
• Hold the explosion
• Replenish dugout stores.
Civic-minded recycling, how does that differ,
    bring the choke-points to collection
points he pokes at groggily,

once more round the block
	shell casings slip & crunch, delivery
systems keep integrity whatever use the spent
	are put towards. A ring-
dove perches in the florid
	Chinese, Persian or an English
orchard as here without number. Cherry
	mess, cherry tat, cherry blossom
stuck like cotton wool overlays year on year
low-level uranium.
			Slung in sentimental waste
			the flesh softens,
			overwrites & overwrites,
			pulses & contributes.

Zealous beside the Arno, Thames, North River,
tippling the Bekaa Valley's finest, scoffing up
stuffed pigeon, slid the layers, keyed in layers
overlay a deep-down Sepulchre, the Alhambra,
Holiday Inn where photographers holed up
receive messages from way uptown, young men
rounded up, having their measurements taken
		end up in the first position,
		high school kids up for it.

Cité Sportif

The flat mandorla pulses painfully beside the basin,
beside Manchester City,
      beside Yankees be-
side deer trainers, NFLP trainers, & at the rim,
about the cindered margin triumph heel to toe
           Cripps trainers,
UDF trainers, Death Row™ trainers,
kangaroo trainers, the personal trainer jabbing this
clipboard, disgusted at practice times:
      So it's *your* personal best
      Would it be impolite to . . .
      Hand the man his photos.
Upon their blocks
beside the washroom, dumb beside running water
poised as though to sip the narcissistic image, skim
new overlays, quaff the syrup water has dispersed—

beside adrenal timing, pineal switch, wire-released
photo-finish, no, not activated, hair-trigger
fingertip control/ is it/ sent the airborne evidence.
How will prints decipher
nor were treads
raised from the crime-scene:
      Cité Sportif,
the scrapbook of unpublished stats, the scrapbook
blows its paper discards across Sabra & Chatila.
Half-screen. For newsprint. High resolution mags.

      Upon their blocks

Get set

Scroll the channels

Switch to surround

In their blanks they squat festooned in bling-bling,
envying wholeness, envying wholeness
recognised in total threat curled round a cider can,
the smart valise, pair of scissors, kindled aggro,
matronly disdain, how dare you third person me!
working out, working out
Personally ensconced in their living-rooms: this
is how life pans away, more or less alleviated,
lagged in the museum of childhood, staring
at vehemence, texting texting above the superbowl,
the shallow blood-filled saucer

Hang about
Hang about

Cité Sportif

Luminance. Slats intermitting despair in particles
voice here throat: resolve goes indigenous. Suppose
master of the ivory gavel beats
                            out irregularities,
musical wire & staves shunt a gated head-to-head
into a dream dwelling into the settlement again,
where are your winged outriders destined for,
the banks, the slats, the terraces, the rows?
        Cheered they may feel
        but by voices
        inlaid below, in ranks
        processed to appear
                paradise or suburb/
                explosion or pressure flask:
you do your best to disperse, they draw you back
in tar lumps, hooded, saying more than you ought,
the stadium power shorted, a cornered, trembling
appellate donned his body-pack, pulling to himself

himself he pitches one more sleight of redemption
face-on in a shadow-press of aides, spins lines
opposite to bulk the open shirt, the broad lapels,
        the bottler, the pressuriser
hauls back in turn,
coach guarantees condition once
led to the changing rooms, found fit, shot:

Cité Sportif.

Embedded in a leaf of slate he passes muster, door
slams behind then is sensed by an unfolding door.
On entry his chargecard was swiped,

his charge sheet scanned.
Houris lounge across power-bumps.
        Receptionist
gesticulates at cool nurse conducting him across
to the cosmeticist. Departing the chair he slides
gold security card,
passport from a range.
        Nothing changes its in-
        scription, its in-numerals,
        its hologram,
        its beneath-the-lines.

A dining club door squelches back to let him pass.
        The greeter glides forward assiduously.
The waiter flurries cloth, accepting him
from the far end, enticed into his personal chair
& re-embodied.
        What
sherbet can I get you, purrs the sommelier,
since you betrayed your folks to get here,
what can I get you to feel, what performances,
what turns
        do you bring to our party?
Dabbing at his mouth with starched napkin, dab-
bing at the spill on the table, blotting his investor's
dress-shirt, dabbing shit, body fluids, sir shall I
put this on your slate for you.

Elevation to Rear Yard

Pathways frost the green field,
spilt traces glitter across the green—
Circuitous but fond
Increased in speed hyperboreally.

Fingers will deposit their originals.
Earth then mount on spikes
or rings. A fleet resonance
compromises the ultra-pure field.

Whereupon clouds pile baffles,
pings confirm paths.
The grasses aver, their gravels
skitter as & where touch loosens.

Otherwise with perfume.
These frittering objects crave life.
What dispels is never derelict.
Cloud assumes but scent

summons the ill-heard object
old, sublet, anew,
sloughing at a hot partition,
moving drumheads being damped.

Trellis

By the walnut grew an apricot,
profligately shading over
courtyard edges. Enter
custodian at mad pelt,

bundles lengths after sorting,
advertises cropped
flames over their marble slats,
containing tremor, earth's

largesse, his being so impatient—
him pink feints divert,
prunus dulcis draws
with polychromatic nods,

cutoff lake, seductive rainbow
fortunately cross-purpose,
outline with a camel
point dabs, dabs pollen.

The entryist forgot why
he ever joined, joined
what—the one step
back he took, demarcates a life-

long position, even in
Tbilisi's heat, his indifference
says more than he thinks.
Pomegranate syrup,

harissa, old railings, breath
fired up evacuates
airy structures, stands enrobed,
surmise becoming rose-like.

Square Dance

Chamfered like mid-eastern
light clench, lets flourish
If I could only. The best frames
for loose knits, carded,

shunt with fruit apostrophes:
spray you being fresh?
Better a lily's horn-tip
browned-off to do me kindness,

for flowering is a premorse
damage: each dire
blossom stamped upon the sky
gathering to retaliate.

People get ready, dabbing
scent behind each ear,
dispensing white organza, tufts
truculent thornbushes.

First Count

'Nothing of sequence or extension'
made of pauses. The big sub-
Saharan emissaries said as much,

waterhole to waterhole. Operant
crowds about that well thirst
licenses, but desert plate by plate

slipped its dash into their number:
A genie, hesitant his step creaks,
combines oil & water, flames
fringing the oases, moloch bulks

forth an incalculable contour,
infill purest quantity, long pause.
Bones won't click or beads cascade.
Sand reversionary to parent store,

bounty thirsting to be crushed out,
one luminary, a pockmarked
disposition knew the sand, a slab.

Trajectory

Re-seat the dislocated stars.
A dry cough mission
pitched a star to whiz,

ribboning among volutes,
down its colonnade;
if daintily it brushed

the disturbed air shook,
however strongly taken
in each breath, scrawled

across pillars: Not Here—
What would you have?
A jetting pinprick,

a violet row of beans,
knock repeating all night
will carry us, signage

withdrawn as premature,
reproached for late;
tremble once in a beady

sprig of a sparrow,
chorus I'd abandoned my
post & revisited my

own setting shamelessly,
like a deck hand
convinced he steers.

Star, hold to course,
turn inside-out, clamp
our latest contrail.

Hear that? disperse it,
a protostar that scurries
mayonnaise, a yellow scud,

or a hollow burnt cask
god, vacating worlds—
the star reiterates here,

& for this other lived
domain, twinkles
in its demise incidentally.

Protractor

Sharp bends & discordant
shake the imperturbable. Fog,
subterranean bars, always
look but sidestep that jump,

jump to it but wouldn't rank
the multi-threaded culture,
can't expect to follow a thread
withholds what it displays.

I break & then dream, re-
gearing, then breaks off. Gent
dressed in a nice three-piece,
bowler, lying toes curled up

before the wall, like a pigeon,
scribble-caught. Never rank
compensates or could infer
Paris Commune, Andalusia—

its colophon looks of a piece
can't be drawn. Throw off
feelers crawl pathways, colour-
code tips were winter cherry.

Writ

Shallying through the slate
clay-divided layers, shift,
the failed threads
blurred & sticking, screw
lodged immovable, re-
employ in lead-windowed
caskets, the tube creatures,
pitiless & loving both,
buried by a trickster lord.

Light may smear or lime
daub profligately, justice
led them forward
to their reserved places
where they have seized up.
Start & the doors
& trunk fly open, ghosts
arrive in managed droves,
manumitted to break

ghosted boulders, pushed
back as an article of faith
to the cold core
of thick crowds of shade.
Or long-buried bodies
jolt to the surface
near where shells explode,
bound over to attend in
booths & sentry boxes,

glass-fronted, get clean
away then stick in what
advantages they take
through giving generously,
grasp in love's prolepsis:
he who never could
do enough, clinched
with one who's biting
tight-lipped his tight wad.
Internally self-regulated.

Multistorey

after Philip Guston

†

Here flooding through hearts' machinations,
pierced rummaging, then were re-bound
to stanch Who did I cut in on this—

heralds though well-motivated pass,
flop round
from cot to school to office, some effluent

spillage a lunar pull shapes, looking helpful
but scarcely nourishes.
Captains want more, they crowd
near to the lacy flaps.
      Earth is stipulating meagrely, cement
sprayed with the gleam of first pressings,
wrinkled sugar-glaze.
                  Yet just a few
crumbs show where the tide was edging to,
treadmarks like admired biography
      readjust condos & streets.
You'll get yours.
The next shelf. Secured assets
turn newsmakers, ours, *no* sweat, brick force.

†

Couriers flash round, parrying with clipped
razor wing ankles, their images below
flock paraselene, now their pure

imagined moon lifts as though
       tides' rejoinder back-
refreshed the used-out sky, biding to coerce,

plough in their strew phosphor;
soil heaves, roses brake, oceans were burning.

Clouds rank the doldrums.
      Shunt billow
Ogosawara Gunto, Sakawan Atoll
              Cloud decelerates:
Hand me my map of these so-called assets —

Cloud hauls them & their trace-loaded swell
rears off the Pacific: aerosol, waterspout.
      On macro level, spoilt fruits,

scavengers, ravenous on every thought level,
scurrying between levels,
          track because

crumbs are what befall, but certain crumbs
      push separate but co-ordinated circ-
ulations through pierced floors,
burning oil rags,
       couriers hot-footing the fire escape

carry unlisted fruit.
Rehydrate with cryptic dew upon re-entry,
this speck, shuck, this integer—
     salients jut from the breached spheres—
glow did it?
               Hand over that gizmo.
               Leave behind those keys.

†

What's that you say? If I've paid for it
why arraign me as dishonest?
Fair enough, fair enough, don't lose your rag.

Rags stuff the flooded chambers of the heart/
block the sluice, torch a granary
        To their bottle bank went all

hugging printed waste, their rag-bound
treadle stumps collect crumbs
up to the open roof. Bird lime, flaky silicate.

        Brake. Manoeuvre. Park.
Pulse-entities of gold asphalt shadow-muted
shuffle round:
        gold butterflies the far prairie,
dolloped from a gas ladle. Sun's
energy feeds & is fed by clipping, chronic
        re-ingestion makes the child
efficiencies above the line, water towers
burn growths in their shadow like pine forest.

& the air-rights stanch, stanch flares:
Private sunset gathering its sphere
studded like a pomander, glamour certificate.

†

Spheres not: composite off-site these baffles
bat their trajectories, knock about,
looping the loop, stomp.

    Entities convulsing orbit, going spare
in a flat spin —
prettify a pink band, one tangerine/
    secures lane discipline,
    secures fiscal climate
ties the embolus up.
        A spiral ramp recoils
to a tracked disk, explosions
tamp down the lunar course, brick on brick.
Prodigious headlines

stack their brick telescope, trained
but useless for viewing. Except spread-eagled.
As though floors were a scrolled archipelago
    massified.
Fetch me my chow,
my pelican chow, chronometric
        What goes on here,
breakers unbreakable, wheat bronze
always, the waterspout drapery totally tanks.

Multistorey

To remember Edward Said

†

Fair's fair & storied is that number you'd first
push against, slippery didn't hurt,
orbiting disconsolately purified. Extra
smart cities plumb the desert, desalinated
     sweat cools our flats
     flatpacked afar,
circular thrall
whips the sand round to enfold our hyperactive
          token kid
teleports his nature through a mauve circle:
First come, we practice
     profile conservation
     archetyping any figure:
Back we report nonetheless & what will be will
What your knees scuff birdlime/
These pads might help
edge along the arch strip, clamp flightdeck/

almost feel assured of the supernumerary being
nifty as to gobble, creative for
     banana ascendant,
     hallelujah peanut brittle
     jam-packed. High-stepping
guards their dung-heap messiness prance over,
walls stand firm & cisterns replenish
on the dot, shit treats the fields,
       bonds mature
     between emplacements
     & holy writ,
     between the settlers &

inflated psalms,
    miraging brick by brick,
green, purple swollen avocadoes stock-
recirculate waters flushing through the carpark.

†

That's not an option, a path is a road is a wall,
fool/ on your way to where?
        Nöosphere
Clouds cycle, pouches bulge
        traits, portraits
Malagasy offcuts.
Ivy drapes had bound the gothic masonry,
        gripping glass,
roots grow disprop-
        ortionate, stems like hairy
millipede to walls, rigmarole.
Tourmaline patrol nails the scumbags.
Driving while black. Drink in cafés while Arab.
Off-road roam the foodstuffs, bleating.
Obstinate the profiles! shall they interrupt
        traffic flow/
cement block.
        A path is a road is a wall is a pen.

No business for you, herder, folder, trader.
Apply for a pass
in a timely, prescribed fashion. Where you go?
        It is restricted access.
Draperies at risk of infestation,
squid, arachnids,
        chitons populate the purses,
wraiths walk
through their sorry fields, heat-
discerned, heat-destroyed.
Military decision. Pin down the chevrette,

pigskin
        rind of calf/
pen ewes' bleats in a service suburb. Time they
turn round & follow their tails or mortify.

Multistorey

For Crying Out Loud

    †

Sleek heralds flap round the table
rectifies the centre of such fuss: its special
cross doesn't exhaust the energy
of the old hillside district they
tooled up to quarantine: kitten-size roaches
      court their sentence,
inattentive hold back the lure or ab-
jectly mumble to pronounce.
Yet the table is disgustingly o'erstrewn
            overdaubed
                  distorted
with what cracks the whip hand,
           charge-
sheet trounce, a nightly hearing
claims its parking spot, flag invincible,
strip system laid over diesel-spotted dirt.
    Admit as evidence hot-
witnessing sarcastic
amici, prosecutors: Sound-
tags flutter in dead space between floors,
          labels make their point,
gull-shrieks of fury, custom-
      crammed between
rubbled minarets & domes,
attend the Eucharistic table shit-splattered.

†

The groundsmen don't get to work
suburban lawns or Las Vegas golfing greens,
dreamt out, unpopulous, aerated,
    these save in jars,
    intensify & trade
flippity-flop awkward through their element,
dried shrimp, dried chillies, the most
adamant of harvests/
    pummelled before men's day
slopes towards their platter
    Praise the stitched-in-time
diligent modernists:
our herald crackles noisily across the seams,
vying for an easily-renewed, daily once
      -off roust-
        about to shrink
indifferently incorp or thistle-
    slide there by glass slide
disembodied city
      never sinus, never shuttle,
definitely fail to clock
    the capsule of release
left in the midden pile like an acorn
of psychoactive stuff.
      Interpreted
to world-wide acclaim & fallout. Aman-
uenses processing its statements
cough out the required
    praise for the choiceless. My gardener
sits alongside me in the bleachers.

Multistorey

Praise Song

†

Praise the benched await their full hearing,
sim unplugged, sim plugged
        Praise the sports bar guys
firm in denial, firm in acclaim
                results
running into bonded sand,
concrete & glass pitch. Who gives a fuck.

Praise bondsmen with the fat green hearts.
Praise the dead loss/
        driving sentiment.
Praise the empanelled
characterising shittiness. A new tract open.
        Commission the new basement.
Indulge their shed time, down time.

Mice with 2μm lesions
startle, chewing out the highway,
this control group seems unperturbed
        maybe little to lose.
                Mice haunching up
brilliant-eyed in warm expensive darkness
        whose folds shake
printed matter forth in its shell-suits,

armoured, animated nubs fur. Fellows,
believe there's some sort of ruckus.
        A blocked trinity looming.
                A defulgence.
That drainoff loss will make water bloom.

Multistorey

after Weegee

†

Leader by detachment not for instance
the socialite will stomach, one brings a lot
liver-rich, now less *haut monde* stomps
Since what they spew by broken
banks, swollen gases, has ordained
one of their number: one of that number
be the straying prince they attend:
       Sighs of a colonist
       escape the pearlised
       moue-mouth: the cap-
acity to love escapes a lucid
bad way to go
clears the sea-lanes—*viz.*
stapled if awaiting, tumbled out
houseboy for those numbers
flocking to the bars after shutdown,
yachting from Long Island: *Grey Goose IV*,
maggotbrain, a soft cage
of point-to-point fatedness:
           His canvas will unwind
to spread the sheet,
     the sheet rise
up to make the sail
           Doing this without stir, the
sheet presides & shall it wrinkle No Sir,
stainless decorates a slack, weary sea,
smoothed over or hydraulic
platform intermediate. Or on the other   -

Belch. There should be high-level
macro study drive a top gallant more brisk
attendance by primitive fowl moult.
Amphorae & coke bottles.

†

There in the shallows lies his subject's body
weed-disguised, hushed up.
Shallows meaning classificatory
knots tease slack/
shallows meaning push-&-pull
substitute for offset intervals from guard
or foul weather flaps:
   browsed, reconnoitred
   soil trampled as this
squishy grove, his attendants gather round
to swing a vehicle's deadlight out in.
Lids vibrate, overprinting swans
lengthen through the narrows.
      She rises filled with gas.
She falls back decorated.
   Hot water pipe
hiss pays its bland tribute, farts & rattles.
Does the flock cause the shoal
shadow underneath?
Does the skein unwind to order
from below?
     We survive as spectators:
boasting high finish, none
affected by her, none really too rough
  What will be will/
unmoving & ungenerous, tripping on its
own tripwires, self-garrotted,
grab the immersed half-recognised shadow:
  Gimme some primitive love.

†

CSI personnel quadrisect a stomped floor,
team leaders set phosphor flares
before truckers/
    Park where that guy says,
haul & stow
the great outside the interior gouges out
then dribbles watery gravel to the ports.
    Blunder cooking pots
tip, stove-in fruit-crates,
tremors holing under the waterline
    Manhattan skyline, New Scotland,
New Britain, irradiated blots
      Pale curious
peridot nor should run its topmost level
ensign through asphyxiating surf
High seas stun up the cetaceans,
giant squid heave & lo! the flexors
beached on tarmac multistoreys, surface
dwellers plunge in skein-nets compensate.

Clear them all out. Clear them all out.
    Shrugs of the consul
    receiving small-arms.
Tawny world stretches for its contraband.
Her mouth dips an oil puddle,
poster-poise flips over onto concrete,
the blow-up little skirt slicks.
    Smudge his mouth like ivy on
toughened glass from inside his sedan,
      his death-throes

watched by car-fulls. Hey slow down.
Hey step on the gas
      Canistered,
sped across the desolate zipcode
paced by out-contracted birds.
Impound the yacht. Spread out the canvas.

Multistorey

after Miles Davis

†

Some litigant through funnel nor
paid-off termless debt
Was it a kind of growth hormone
      Now consider
shower stops, holds, directs its brain-
storm then launches
at a compact *fait accompli*, busts
What are you thinking of. The last
enricher of the signed, codicil
some flier might have
been let skim, secretively
funnelling light, responds
to an earlier project now sleepy,
      might once soar
      furiously relaxed, but floats
above his destination's
riff or vamp, black magus
As though he had encompassed it
before setting out.
Took unawares by such prescience.

Some flier feathering his nest,
flying to confirm his abstract range,
glides/ hangs loose
on air sagging (swoon)
      that re-slides
below his stricken indecisive
chest Yet indecision proved effective
in embrace, then a system,
      locked as a stylite updraft

hedges round this plain tightly,
aquifers tripped by shadow
gurgled their response,
        little springs played guileless.
Now the integrity of winds
grapples stars & ocean-
floor events That's how it pans out:
Now the integrity of rock
Integrity of the gnat's course
        what-you-will
        sniffs round:
their stuck-up integrity
plundering the biosphere,
rolls the thin mantle to a lump sum.

Multistorey

For Heaven's Sake

†

Accessed through albedo fuming thickly
    tucked over sky
always rests beneath its total thought,
post-dated in the sky's voiding of a myriad
unsupported birds,
my brother dragged beside his
deeps, re-staging them
        Go forth & multiply
in time for lot authorities to pack
    Pinch stopper. Ramped layer on layer
adjusts them this space,
decks them in certificates & feedback.
    Stars twinkle underneath.
What do stars deliver? Stars
dig in, they disclaim to his beseeching face
        ever having,
ever having sent one plummet,
burst one rocket, once heaved or erupted.

†

Tabled on that face, flickers like a glider's
breaking shadow disarrays dogs'
jostle, recombined in packs,
joining dots to knit a continent
    cross-
totality, cross the sky was now the barque
of the low heat muffle's rolling up.
Ants & roaches alternate with doppler
    wheatwalls advance—
the biomass, the high society
    marches into wheatwalls,
carries petrol cans.
What can he discern in the lurid light?
Ours the weight,
        don't let fumes addle,
fixed intent will photosynthesise—
    Digest.
    Drive on up. Flocks of birds cross.
Why it's preparatory. Cans rattle.
    The dogs have gone to the country.
    The country goes to blazes.
Hot nubs rush out from the wheatwalls.

†

Twin lead-out wires, the blisters on this
sub-chassis, air thins,
        the gate flag ripples,
plasma shadowed by angelic body-bits,
electron lilies take less than time:
carbon sheaves can't
disfigure now the blue's unvarying,
& the vertical bearing cage is but grass.
            Brother Wolf:
Already I'll feel dint. Or strop.
Broke the lead in his pencil.
    Strategically allied to
cable-runs were sex investors, bandage
dangly bits or loom interminable
        tucked back must weave
in bored arousal, not yet dead Excuse me.
        Penultimatum.
I can't remember my car. Blue? Toasted?
Brave in the pearliest dawn on deck
        turning over uncomplaining.

†

Carbon put-on, poor excuse for a human,
      fed & watered, synchronised,
sternly cropped from the one threw
         timing out,
                  itinerary
for each flatbed judders, carbon rags
loudly differ more the less they vary:
      Brother brother brother
What's going on.
                   Refugees
pay per view, crannying the site of
a refectory, monastic fish-pool,
ballistics testing-bed —
      undeterred, each refugee
making out, gets *its*,
& its, its printed T-shirt, its word-hood
proclaims:

step on the gas, hutches make the human
roadside, the ground-down sub-
      aqueous particle
click into alignment. Inspection pit.
React at once: Proceed to level three.
            Refugees
scattered on the lawn with tools,
        within their brackets shrug:

only phi effect unites these brothers,
a pluripresent movement
rocking them from foot to foot.
    Happy birthday.
Time to put the lid back on this ruin.

†

Crunchy wing-cases, drifty fungus spores,
a moth evades a web in a slipped burst,
         usual crooked toe, a Roman
nose, stooped, suggests a coprophage in
muddy prints, scales to city
district to transit hub, taxi, bus,
                          ledges up.
On clenched lids overlaying bluetop,
         bonded flakes, lattice bliss.
Yes top of the morning's
bluish cloth pressing down full adhesion
so to lift successive floors.
         Prefabric. Denimode. Two

taurid demons trapped inside a compact,
desperate for the open, steer
faithful to a grooved seam, jerked about
with cross-scarring
         racking up the points
through quags of magma,
locked mesmerically on ramshackle
satellites, dangerous cans,
         where did they hi-tail, tangle
at what level — deck one?
         Skinny fuckers do whatever. Giant
squid outweigh the ground's grand total.
                   Obscure volcanic ash puff

straggles out in days. The casings tumble,
brothers flop beside a gleaming mound,
              gone to earth,
         turnip-heads laid up, cucumber
slices on their eyes.
Acquisitions & what fuels
kicks the transmission train, trucks dispel
         blabber shadows, moiré
from inceiving: load the decked-out
groaning board, obese gods strip
their tripes & suck marrow.
Gulls launch off the concrete ledges,
         headlong swooping down to blazes.

Visitors

Wait their verdict, stop all leaks,
the verdict will put an end to speculation.

We put our hands to it compliantly,
reconstruct before the first build module,

marked up, Lloyds of London value,
value added to set term for all dispute, this

knows its stuff & how its stuff plays:

A core policy, a key principle,
stampeding pack shook a doorjamb verdict.

Frittering to a purpose, breathing heavily,

dominant white couple are into clingfilm.
Not one drop will waste.
                            Like lemurs,
oil droplets spin named & docketed.

Architecture

Vegetative imps will grow &
people the dead-centred empyrean,
sheet on sheet of clear
cartilage, their scuba bubbles

battering against the feathered
clear thatch. After
& despite such devices, airbrushes
cap it all, glistening & frictionless

tag the watery house
should have been maintained
pince. Sometimes I am unfeeling,
sometime love to folly,

or like onion skin, slip.
The vision is air amounts
to an egg throne, the fly-by-night
communicate on love's leash.

Scamp

Intersections red earth
Stop:Go grinds
Their slam-typical flouts

gut-stuffed sofas, cups
& buckets, satellite dishes,
automatic firearms,

ridge dogs, ridge vines,
cucumbers.
Go with full cover
crunch dreamily & float

self cutting into self,
most revert acceptingly
into colour ground.
Red earth blinds.

Stumble

Reinstall ff.,
mouth on its
fatal branch, buff
uniaxial the damaged

beak below
stairs, there is no
group attainable
to unthinking service,

pointless feet
& fingers fidget,
guidance systems
scratch, embed, fray.

Bind them back in,
as memory does
matted tubers,

net the starry
dome of flight-paths,
reinvent prec..

Claim (tlc)

Left-eye, left-eye left in Honduras,
then big man working top of his valley,
shiny coffins didn't coop, turn them
up enshrined in a clause. Leaving

more than we calculate. If iceberg
lettuce flew the skies with a 1950s
phallic confidence, shrunk pain;
if high speed collisions, felt in the gut,

claims on paper, claims in blood,
sacred soil on bloody soil on sacred;
if the spores of harm would condense
flesh opaque or regionalised till now,

work through like shrapnel stars
blanket innocence mapped & so
malign with celery, peppers, apples,
white land cubed, oedematous blank,

the blank of roamed skies: Yes—

returning herdsmen woke the pioneer,
a precedent underwrote his claim,
riddling yellow sheaf & boxwood,
consuming his liver, did for her too.

The claim covers the skies.
        The claim was drawn up.
The claim is dirt.
The claim extends down to the centre.

Electrolysis

Mush, by high heaven legalised
following front-end-load, & truffles
enveloped, had their fringes only

taking after the father, such luxuries
Jupiter's halls never hoarded,
I'll stitch your arsehole, instinct

hurtles downwards, too-abrupt its
shaft rolls, columns the mats'
apologies for billowy clouds:

your fortune mauled Thursday,
add back then you wouldn't notice,
pumping air to bursting, stack

its bargain basement, floorless
heretofore. Opportunity will bust
its tympanum, the solidifying

light clumps & bulks, tapioca
gobs in cherryade, a syllabub
thinks up cloud, thinks interference

lightning-lit, carries huge ideas.
Air had been fertilized, if thunder
calves its squares of prostrate

curiosities flopping the mats—
ritually absolved, they'll leave
in squadrons a malodorous lake—

soon they fight for one breath.
Seagulls screeched at their approach
ScrewYou ScrewYou ScrewYou.

Step by Step

Star-creases re-run themselves on the sky,
puckerings about knots of time lapsed
repeat; crows hang their murder bells
from time to time & in other branches.

Shamed figures taunted by implacable
cables of shine, shamed figures drift
with no comment, no reflection, each
clutches his or her open or unopened bag.

The patterns fall again, to same effect.
A blow in the face, a vicious thrust
learnt by accident carries on by ricochet.
Sustained in collapse the metal writhes,

windows fall in, their brilliant squares
land before the feet of the most damaged.
Stay with this language, hear its echo
over the years ring into a previous echo,

toe-taste a footfall into that acoustic
shame louvers, cables sing, the red tower
squats foundations, caves undervaults.
The grey escalator breaks, breaks, lifts

grey teeth biting through their comb shoe.

Leda

Tabled, like the back-thrust of a sharp
intake would be the spread
they had been promised, snap petals
off before chancing to open.

Coldshoulder might have them licked
but indissolubly. Wild types
shake off loose approximations,
then decide for the air, are buffeted

above where some picnic,
these enjoying that the tempo
obliges to champion. Once oscillating
they'll know to want a flared gust

sweeps the board. Objects
scaling down, reciprocators
hydra-headed lurch back & whack
hard against the diaphragm they spasm.

Even so, a hinged egg slung beneath
trails from its pucker, threads to follow
for the overcorrect guest
all that white flock will turn from.

Iphigenia

A different line gives & takes & plays,
corded with lines of flight.
At outset
Out of errancy
lines of flight deviate from loaded flightpaths;
     & down a perplexed line,
some further line off our intended furrow
lags, resumes,
         detours ahead,
jerks & leaves its knots to hang in the air,
stratified cloud-cuckoo-land.
     Small wonder working upwards,
willing a definite line as though destined,
tied knots to play free,
         infinitely braiding,
     plans yet oppress the ground.

Cars snort openly & pull out.
Subways shudder, doors open. Dead names
crowd, carpet, stuff, upholster,
     piling it on thick
puffy quilted asphalt, napped concrete, trees
traumatised to mop-heads.
Wayward
bulk
encumbers the field.
         A four-hour window
lag sickens,
lagging plugs the aperture, lint rises:
     stars decompensate & light breaks

a Western grant to be overrun
triple determines some thick curtaining
of ours,
                        hidden title,
            as pleating or laceration wouldn't.

Exact reflection blots out the original
A beam does not break but self-expunges
            Too much intensifier.
To be imperial hub
                        Come in, Come in,
multiplying, stuttering,
touches down with flocking copied escorts.
Stretch. Insert conduit.
Checksum.
Verify.
            Inaugurate a line of inquiry
blinds itself in childhood ullage, summons
Brillo Pads, Pritt-sticks,
            Brylcreem, mercury pomade,
The Popular Ford new-fledged.
                        Calculated smash.
Objects shorting overhead power-lines.
                        Cavity wall wires

Whose loaded grid shocks tightly distances,
trailing through side-doors & traps,
                        blockhouses, emplacements:
These cross-hatchings are its doing,

flipping open flaps, tiptoeing on brutal
    architecture,
finding spaces, winces.
    Considering the clip he goes,
basements rattle wide,
brother fortress
sticking out its siege of flying machines
        opens from within.
He sticks this for as long as viable.
                Walk & squawk.
Then he scrams in his new car
raising bright sleepless welts.

But the real work precedes such symptoms.
    Small wonder looking round—
             trailing edges,
paddles, slapping upwards like true selves
off the fattening surface—
smack each goes into the bulk drink,
    downed repeatedly,
    screw-tight,
shatter their own approach & first glimpses.
In cages in the basement
the illegals prepare food.

They conceal the turn, beyond the fast bends
or the slow bends, their blind turn granulates
economically, why the guardians are shutters!
light's held by them for congested objects

slotted between these boards: caparisoned
with beads of envy, stitches of dependency,
these are the most we have, our flicker book.

Iphigenia

You might untie a boat,

thereby slip down the lit
slipway into animate darkness,
waders drop from boltholes: down in the pit,
in the pen a hard silence,
        but this wind
through soughing willows has no remedy
it might turn to;
Haitian, Bangladeshi memories rock
treetops, floodplains can absorb no more
        habits of flesh,
            monsoons reach Montana,

                helicopters

faltering over their long-awaited patch.
They had been so long upheld
singly without knowing by these portions let
loose when designated:
        The deed applies to this grant only
        Inasmuch to risk the deed
aftermath
post hoc
the loaded phrase will have extended,
section files pressed into the deed as lines/
cordite puffs
between the outcrops
        so glum hardly worth
such slogging effort.

Toll worth its deed, contumely,
  charge worth the phrase,
signalling clearance to our helicopters
sprout in their millions on salt pads,
raising dirt from every tuck,
raising dirt from every pocket.

  Simply put

this porcine para snarls at skinnies: Go! Go!
Fridges slosh suburban quarry tiles,
offloading their concealed
    lit topslice from obese
    earth, self-inculcated

  Don't leave it capped.
A shaking hand brings a taper.

Push off, push into the spate

Peer out. The twin town, the flower
    The swollen race
          Act now!
Slide down the bank softening,
dropped on the outskirts back of the rig,
chewing dirt
    The worst terrain
to vanish inside, you slam against a retaining
wall, a windbreak muscles up in thorns,
dikes impede you,

testing fields grip ankles
Black earth, littered with brassica roots,
clumps bleeding feet
            Voracious gulls.
Scabby earth thaws in thready light
infiltrating along its waterways.

Iphigenia

The while maimed habit pulls the light cord,
shadows cast forward & backward
thickly off the hinges,
     old country's gangs
play on its foretellableness, bend
back with final snap repeating
lemon liqueur, mint tea,
blinis, betel. Filed
streamers, feathers gripped in the fist,
     cloud magnificence,
     visible signs made fixtures,
     gross vestige company—
     Be still,
lighten the panelled meadows, redeploy
the crabbed files to the outermost
wisps of presence—

     Compass-hauled I still
this near delinquent sky once I have sponged
expressions
off its slate,
          wiped off scribbles,
perversely slack
     traceries feebling faithfulness,
burning with split lip, chewing out stray
diligent paths & plans
     wandering re-
capitulates, re-scores,
     captures. Though I still
say, this is the place
spoken of & named, won't I still
clap the boards, report for my signing off,

clap the boards about a concrete bed.
                    Submitted flight-
plans having cleared
in bundles I shall enter them,
drill as though trepanning. Pastoral flutes
bore a thousand filaments.
Fasces.
Nazi occupied chateau.
        Air smells as it did in the Alps,
vapour erases valleys.
        No-mans-land abuzz
        Command plus
                Connect plus
        Forward battery
pins me down in a defile, pounds into carbon
shies the ferny tracer,
                reconciles at the hippocampus
errant halo
Larks, finches
choke their flight simulator, crash
feathery at the real threshold. Still
do what I expect of myself, still play turncoat.
                        Dutiful descant.

The material mind
won't weaken.
Events fall out just so.
The event shrinks from the necessary thought.
        Centre-stage but pluralling.

By pulling the cord I activate my manager,
                by this choice I hinge,

an elaborate structured emptiness
yawns heavily.
I have responded within 14 days,
I have responded,
        promptly claim my no-commitment
trial of a mute cookie.
The sentence is delayed hunger.
The rocks put on weight.
        Mud gets more muddy.
        Trails tangle & stiffen.

Iphigenia

They rigidify the airy squint, raise ocean
with their frothy blood, even the rocks swell
horrified, why the dead are not ghostly!
but contract to make more of flimsy projects.
We ply between economies: fixed rates
feed upon us & we feed on mucky fields,
our recompense the overabundance that presses.

Get on board now, get in, help up your father
on the gang-walk,
plenty bucks & welters below.
Twist one string so mother suffocates,
bandaged in enormous vestments.
      Or was it mother rolled
her corded sky-hanging of her own volition,
tropical print:

The wider-eyed her face, the heavier gauge
clouds a sky foregathering, one
overcast, one trashy-thatched,
loaded, hedge-trades to cover loss,
preoccupied with prospects for bottling plants,
      quick-assembled
      starter yeast, line operatives,
      interviewing temps, inter-agency—

slotted slickly in padded courts
fit for the sty's wallow, airy, rainy pellets,
           pasture preparing patties.
It's by such stockbreeding
cords play productively, a womb throws
bobbins into the tight courts,

into the padded breach:
        follow the storyline, delineate
the thread to where its hammock is swinging,

chase the story to a steroid pumped corpse
stripped & handsome,
surpassing use.
Chest-punctures bubble. Casting adjusts
snow flurries with the leaf plummets' tapping,
        bright flakes draw feeder lines,
        draw untangled harness,
small change through sorter trays
jiggles, stays in circulation, demands its cut,
spangled print.

For this will pay well. Confidants of the family,
        consiglieri
bulk out each to the ideal puff of vapour,
rolling through the sun's dip,
sip Krug, savouring Osetra
                watch field slaves
break aside in demurrage, lose the plot,
what complicates them? squatting on ankles,
time suspended rankles on their backs.

They defy the airy squint, curse the departed
from dehydrated mouths, the natural world un-
sockets from the social, god showing countenance
as though that would abash mastery. What?

A working day lengthens whatever is produced,
the ghosts of the dead drive machines
beautifully-engineered to collect the blood needed.

An unconditional line spools & wires
cross & at each junction with their wasted gifts
stand the resourceless:
failure is their set vocation, fail neatly, proof
not arrived-at but substantial in the frame
not entered but keyed,
      spiders them in stretch harness
propagates like knot-weed,
emphysema kelp.

Iphigenia

Visited on barley sugar barley water barley wine
     barley whoreson,
O barley cane John Barleycorn
Swollen in his coat he transubstantiates fume.
                Lemon barley.
Whisky.
In this way the small grain gains bulk.

Starch fuels the floating factories'
     misbegetting
microphytic fronds hyper-propagate, block
any exit,
spiralling through vinegar,
thicken at the base of the alembic
     Thus too the surface creams & spumes.

Internal welts crimsoning, their congealed crime
     riveted each button door,
where yeast the human analogue, its cells'
limitations switching off, carcinogenic
floaters on Burgundy,
            performs wheelies, jack-knifes,
rides the premonition, rides before it curls
into cascade.

Every proposition swells, birthing clingy scarfs,
a jellyfish's lunar pulse.
The destroyers are fabulous too.
     I love the cars
     I love the cars
Whitening on the bench. The centrifuge.
The little fridge.

The strips of yeast cells as they stalk the earth.
    I love cigarettes.

Others snack on fattening rations, lifts rise
& plunge at one finger. Caged within music
they greet travellers, these our apparitions,
accruing light to us with retail cheer,
revel in such grocers' generosity, their con-
summate fervour. Using market movements
we invent new snacks for them, broker Fausts.

I like it sweet, I like it whipped, I like it salted,
    I like it fresh-churned.
Does the rose bush burnt from pure longing
    visited with fire rust,
transfigure in the blaze to the same figure?
The same shall furl & pack fire
into its prolific heads,
& does the blood-red garland
    decked in thorns like spurs,

manifest the crowning dream of a virgin
wading through blood—Don't fuck with me:
I want the thick cultivar.
The sentence is delayed hunger.

Iphigenia

Shallow sphinx:
Untie the boat, launch with cloud-dwellers
rafts where lines finagle off-
handed, flick
        taunting
short of the air-grabbing hand,
lightning wanders & the moderate fasces
fall in general.
O you got green eyes o you got blue eyes O
        you got grey eyes
Flatten me too, confuse me.

        At 7 a.m., hour of the smokers
Régie Turque, Passing Clouds
                Rollup paper tears on the lip
on a bus out from Exeter,
yes you got hens teeth yes a blue moon/
        milk & honey.
Just like at 8pm kids elbow past,
                tastes
flap against the rocks & pools,
        Pickapeppa sauce on a barley fryup.
Clash City Rockers meet Deleuze '78
scenting moods like rooms,
scenting old rooms like moods,
roaming their slots.

Come the bath is salted.
Come the air fills with Ninjas.
Flatten knots into the limelight strings:
        Gossamer whips

leave off wrapping chrysalises.
Seeds hang in the cavities in the bath loofa,
                    swelling.
Yes every ventricle hides a new toy.
          The city
welters with blood when toys are seized.

Saddle meagre poleaxed.

                    Helicopters
stitch along the seams of a rifted
self-dormition, Parlophone, Tamla-Motown.

Shallow sphinx,
immune & free from all stain,
is it your whisper twists against my skin,
          each little status light blinking?
Snakes float in the muddy floodwater.
          I am eating too wildly
          I devour.
The dead too are sick from delayed hunger.

Iphigenia

Pitching or becalmed, head for that outcrop.
          Steadily she goes at hazard
shakes & cracks the slate
atlantic board & proving ground.
Sharp change of course, whose cant
a pilot reconciles,
          jockeying the chopper
through twin buttresses/ Hang on in
          High stakes players
vomit, slump on deck, drain power.
We played for the beheld sign
but dropped a bundle.
Terraform the asset earth on fractal outcrops.

A parsec would flood their outgoings. Crops
produce only indigestible trash,
          mortality is mocked
by lumps beneath each chair each papa
was ensconced on.
                    Open positions
fared poorly, picked off
data rummage, picked off squawk box,
          picked off instruction,
left marooned in the fateful bracket
swapping parts they need, stuck on outcrops.
Like so,

cutting each surmounter his slack. Scheduled
as his flight chases westward,
undercover agents & débridement

prepare a landing pad, doling
      sachet heaven—
harps in the countryside, simplicity,
paeans to the perfected thread.
Blood teems, a fixed thought
releases its myriad.
Over slow granite creep, out of exile,
      whirring eidetics
tilt into formation, flicker
mapped against these cloud-girded outcrops.

Iphigenia

Queen of ships, chopper queen
Benign reaper,
        Cast your reproving look,
reinstate history, free
wheels, lines, drawing out their implications.

Any throwing his foolish spool
chancily, snatching clothes
      draped with each morning,
plays directly to her hand shot out for fate's
      completer/finisher:

The thin rich
tread their uncoupled mills,
the sore poor children of some substance
shake shocked to eyes exposing them, behind
bust screens in trailers,
      garb hurriedly:

Weight, cranked by much of less,
boosted competitively,
      toils choked water lapping
hurt amid serpents
dropped in sequence from the synaptic ledge,

      credulous,
kneels to an obedient castle, it too tallies—
Before she snags the line in front
      for a neck-tie, a vein-tie,
tussles to rise free of swelling, garrulous stone.

Queen of ships, in your praise she swells.
Queen of tumescent emptiness.

Home workers join in prayer at dusk, pins
bristle from tight mouths. Field servants
buckle-to; whose work, a watery surplus,
keeps body & soul together, but not theirs,
pre-dispensing any store they'd set aside—
While a smart enzyme from their trash,
traded on Chicago Futures, makes fortunes.

Chopper queen, lay the ground.
        Scorched earth bloats.
Subsidiaries have hived off, clumped off,
chasing their profit,
                revenants
shifting like the shadows overlap bellied urns.
Grease sapphire must be splurged
then the table drain,
the floor run like pulp pressing out paper,
        trickle whey, grappa:
blot the malingerers, mop them up,
their fatty clouds can pile & drip with dawns,

they need the dawn but we distil,
they need bulk but we want cars.

Get back on board, spoilt, frisked & fevered.
Again the forebears plough ahead,
        cannibalised

in generous sweets, botox lips,
applying handles, thicken tongues.

Queen of angular heaven,
draw the line against these.

Benign reaper, all inherit.
Riffle out the deeds for this stake,
       they shall layer
like a reverse autopsy,
a back-handed archaeology restuffs the earth,
the puffy black & dark blue of poverty,
       thick soles.

They rigidify the airy squint, raise ocean
with their frothy blood, even the rocks swell
horrified, why the dead are not ghostly!
but the cellulite bulking out flimsy projects.
We ply between economies: fixed rates
feed upon us & we feed on mucky fields,
our recompense the overabundance that presses.

The Shoal of the Ditto Ship

for Miles Champion

'One day he'll wake with wings'

Or fixed gaze in vitro intro-
spects, centipeded they get tied
up through reefs, or riffing
smattered off the obtuse bulk
cast away legless, their cousin
vaguely wagged, illuminated
pillows of puff, much touch
dodges being dwelt-on or
arrived-at Must I peel or empty?
Teflon Ted Whatever you say
dangles like a benediction.
Twinkletoes, your scarlessness
locks the scarlet under skin,
as shame were that shame
brought up to its own mark,
then all is trussed & shut,
sealed off like a marshmallow
butterfingered bare choir. Reef
Tom to arrive at certainty,
veer not, shy off or scatter,
vent not the stacks imbibing
vapour sustenance, would
these package deal finickers
down within the voided grates,
cap them, since their terminus,
playing to their divisions,
plugs the too-routine leaks.
This mush dons his quizzical,
this plate gurns, Robert this

Meissen figure, peregrinating
slashes in my baked Alaska,
periodic or wedge flume
carbon remnant, *primus inter
pares* cloaks in citizenship—
Coney Island Russian taxi,
Chinese pin-pursed laundress
TriBeCa Bridge? Your ID!
The order stops the tracks of
fleet Helvetians, Swiss pixies
mobilising legs with dream,
discourage cramp, patch nerves
euplastically, re-set their bones.
Leaning from her saddle, wee
Titania can bestow a blessing,
dabbing dry the dropsical,
easing crooks if struck rigid,
draws down the flues, follows
into the cold-box or cream
bowl, horseflies in harness
tugging behind The Upsetter.
Clip Clop Clippity Clippity Hi:
deer tics bring lime disease,
mosquitoes siphon West Nile.
Clip Clop Clippity Clippity Hi:
fireflies bale their thistledown
bolsters, mop up leftovers,
squall bruising cloud edges,
cobalt-skirt their huff & puff
flushes chimneys, vaccinates
household staff, hauls along
Maria, Li, Primrose, Naomi,

Sam's personal trainer, kids
at school you were dwarfed by
were shaken by a choice phrase
filling a salience landscape;
penguins of your cloud buttes,
behind-the-arras prompters
cracking their tush knuckles
shrink flaunted words to size,
bearing up too-complicated
knees in alcoves, squinnying
heaps of bone, a coffin clutch
of gladsome bone mounted
on his pillow, femurs guide
the galumphing litho press
mashing its diacritical trickle.
Girl you really got me now
You got me so I can't die.
The ravenous ghosts constrict
thin pipes with sucking-up,
craving eats from his big toe
looming over a fire-ant army—
O fallen arches O articulacy!
a kick in the hand stubs a bush,
fiddle-faddle strewn-about
pudency stamp. *You're too rude*
you rake, you fop, you mohawk,
you with your fab nose-bone.
Luke reeling at such vileness,
stashes books on a hearthstone
overnight, in hemp baloney,
cleans up his act & itemises:
Gilgamesh perks up on cue,

Ulysses as per usual curious,
Malmude packing his boxes
for the proverbial little press.
The inner cerecloth shrinks
chaldean, root-fanned stylus
pokes into these roe deposits,
gripped in icy fingers ticks
micro-level duplicates—How
can they endure the light,
these vulnerable figures? How
did glaciers wobble like airships?
chains pup a consequence?
leave no stain on its envelope?
misfolded, misfolded, proof
against tears, against semen,
paid in full but fallen short,
capturing a torpid substrate
prickling where the low cloud
muzzles against their moss-
sopped cocoons against the sky,
misfolded to indestructibility,
glitching up the brain stem.
None of the above applies
None of the above follows
without receptor sites signal
strapping their cuneiform,
vaporise through mesh, honey
welling between their wires,
evenly eventless dropper filled
but long in the tooth, bony,
scribbled like a slut tornado
searches for its porch & picket.

Do I see Johnny Appleseed?
Was that my casual gunslinger
reels on the deck with kuru,
holding forth & misfolded,
sought to expiate his triggers,
triggers of the small mercies?
A novel variant stirs the rank
antibodies, you must be you,
snails, smearing, butt-naked,
visibly, despicably ambitious,
hauls over the icecap its satchel
stuffed with props to scale
Just add water, quietly steam
while the felt thickens, furs,
buckles in intelligent tucks—
promise you'll look beautiful,
promise an eyeful gratifies
Scottie's scopophilia, minions
crushed by the saint system,
stripped by Lilliputians,
bring me my Negroni, swoosh!
Clouds mouth a new dawn,
records skate, a sumptuous
troop, refolding tallied initials,
promenades across the whole-
earth mercator. Avenue A
clouds gush vodka, vivid
pangs chase after shredded fish,
roast guinea pigs & tripe:
Felipe, I'll have your selection,
the polymerised sweet cells
defend their right to adapt!

animate the dynastic pods,
leprechauns, a flea circus
climbing a prandial trapeze,
ribbons & spirals, lamellae,
locusts & the leaf-cutter ants,
defend their right to adapt!
Slurping at dab nectar, woozy
comforters fall, denied access
by these fibrous bunches
spongiform at base—hey,
you trying to stick your nose—
Know what's coming to you?—
Say you pass the horseradish
clockwise while at home?
Insolent to waiters? Get lost!
Ouch! ouch! An apt little hound
rounds up misdeeds in flocks,
water thickens with tadpole-
dense performances, frogs
are hopping on marked paths.
Leander swims, Meander strays,
the very trout who gasped
for oxygen in a stock-pond,
wallow on the sludgy floor.
Clip Clop Clippity Clippity Hi
puts spurs into the cladogram,
dispersing those top dogs
long solitude had made weird
Like a lemur. Or a marsupial
frolics onto a new reserve,
a positive fit, a vacuum seal,
a win-win trade. So why do

shrunken heads find boughs
peeking out of the manholes,
did crowbars & indigenes
blow the cover rising to cover
the cover I cover myself,
unscarred cover with scarlet,
steal the proto-immersible,
insinuate this endoscope?
authorise the brain scan?
I was a rush of released mice,
roaches from under the sink
advancing through Sullivan St,
milling towards a hot ticket
cupcake, where's Vesuvio?
That brass tocsin animates
the grave-figures, bony fringe
defiling out, nano-machines
rafting the capillaries, rush
to rows appointed, terror tots
pullulate in their gung ho.
Bees swarm from Broadway.
Michelangelo. Minihaha. Blink.
Pictures of matchstick men
& me & me & me. Ticklish
midget submariners giggle.
Fireflies whirr. The pestilent
cockchafers, shrunk to tiny
whisks gad round the sewers,
household gods gape & gulp,
emulsify where sore necks &
sumps lift up their gates, O
helicobacters mass in the gut

like Apocalypse Next. Meet
Princess Bianca. Magdalehna.
Cut. Shut this trap, mother.
Consider the hands shake.
Consider this shaking hand.
Mine re-strap, thought-over,
others pull in adverse ranks,
some more habit-spatulate
from days & nights tunnelling,
skirted round or blew apart,
screwed sinuses or undercut:
these subverting their class,
that dumbcluck I had drabbled
lurking to buttonhole me,
came bushy-tailed if whistled
forward, wrenching my lapels,
brought all kinds of baggage.
Palsied hands. Featherbrain.
Chills, cracks. Frost ossuary
Dark place where seven roads
resurfaced. Kiln. Or broiler.
I am the god of hell's cold
fracturing the shut-down
grate, lithium console calms,
smoke like an iced margarita
quenched the chimney roar,
their camisole stood legless,
bones laid out to feed the fire
devastated, sparked a sub-
zero disaster, frozen gushers
flaring back to cloud cover,
flaring round the polar vault,

snapped in a cold clamshell:
splintered were its runnels
lifting swollen tongues. Over
the hearth's slate, jumbled
quartz plectrums, carved ivory,
burnt corks, pipe dottle of
gone companions, vagabonds,
boozed, spat, freely caroused
below the roof-tree, DNA-
analysed chattels, bony shards,
shades of powerful clothing,
room is right, curse in order,
amulet & gold brooch check,
your details have been verified.
To such a desecrated altar
decorators prance, slubbing
plaster over the pancreator,
fret walls in pernickety grids,
crematorium pigeon holes:
To this end, to this zilch,
the great cheese, the sponge,
a destroyed coral collective
petrifies anew its every unit
incubates local pathogens:
Clip Clop Clippity Clippity Hi/
egg cartons hatch by module,
sash windows rattle tinnily,
sheets of cellular wax bulge
each with a miniature nob
thrust half-way out, squishy,
pinky-grey & ready to slide
about its tumefacient work—

going down to alphabet street,
white boys cruising sidewalks
jut their hips, the parasites,
dark shadees, parodies, trans-
formers, topers, those fore-
runners snacking on decoded
Pekinese, Peruvian bites,
Babylon perchance or Sumer
Check their chiselled teeth.
Verify the funerary figures,
terracotta sightless, armless,
faceless comedia of excess,
the whole shebang, the circus
marches out of a mausoleum:
Here the autobots shall dock,
senseless, gold-connected, clad
in memory-woven denim,
dishes bright, whips aquiver,
scout above eye-level, sweep.
Here advance the autobots,
exiled from a bright matrix,
gathered in choice skin, dis-
avowed but in chameleon
lock with the old regiment
spirting gravel, grating nerves,
crank till a cylinder aligns,
wriggle on prepared sheaths.
I, I'm just a little tin soldier.
Walkin' talkin' livin' plug.
Needles & pins. Neologisms.
A mensch on a bender, Jack
on an even keel, shameless,

shambling like an autobiotic
through a fuckpad boneyard,
remedied in shreds & patches
burns out of the marrow.
You, Scarbo! You, Ondine!
Consuela, mollusc was your
foul mouth & your kindness
jabbering on my private bits,
Augustus, your melodica
ricochets but courses through
the massive resistant sheets,
Moran, the night has no parts,
that's because you're asleep,
the fate of the crew of the
Alioth waits to be disclosed,
shaken from its bubble tissue,
seraphic heads blow shanties
smart as paint, & briskly
shine their epaulettes, medals
paving their hearts, crunch!
splinter under the die-stamp,
suborned swords of elves
hack vehemently where fringe
solder, shaving the spilt tin,
palsies down like beer-tops.
Panda-eyed the cherubs blub
all over semi-demi-hemis,
tonsured bobble heads each
sailor hallmarked with his year,
circular scrolling calendar
predicts little volcanoes, shock-
wave oceans & the hesperides,

blue cascades of numerology
sluicing over the span, men
& women cropped & slotted
each in her cellular conclave,
the way we expect love to be,
reverberates, a leaden cavalry
decorated, bodhisattvas,
pure land guardians practice
circular breathing, lit mandala
starts spinning, its imp-chain
of blue bone, sore distended
stomachs & necks squeeze,
battering fans like cockchafers,
whirring gods. Bones, dust,
millipedes in a single cohort,
amulets endowed with multi-
access, nub-end top-knot
yogic flights rehearse, sponsor
an ethereal choir of gnats:
Clip Clop Clippity Clippity Hi,
the clog dance of caterpillars
avid for internal burn & crawl.
Of heldness and of caresses you
have become the entrepreneur.
Inside me was this longing
which did not belong. Nests
of beetles stir, jewel-like frogs.

Thelonius

Flies muck around the worktops,
rip-light aeroplanes
    scribble outside,
depositing their threads in summer only.

Morning's drone, dragging thicker bands,
protect it shall this summer
    uneventfulness,
depositing its corners, brilliantly

sharp corners. Others would simply float
through their vocals, wag lordly
tongues collecting pollen—
    a ticket, a tasket—

Flies muck around the worktops,
slapped down beside a
take on whose hip home, don't
    Crash apposition, like that stoic

aerosols light propulsion, stand for it—
Scroll multiplayers don't skip, never stop
    They are sustained
final flourish mounts in cadenza,

ostinato, ostinato, the slow hand keeps
stride, a celebratory dinner/
    flaunts his necktie cutely dunked
iridescent back section.

Flies muck around the worktops,
find a hole to bunker in, nektonic,
scribble unfazed
facings like the gift that finds its 3rd & 4th

covenanter, placeman, corsair—
Indument
surroundsound zips above the over-plush,
depositing its fly major minor

wraps it up that footsie-play & holds
Hold it there. Tonic
clunk. Holland Tunnel. Ostracon Bridge.
Rev counter busted his stride.

    †

Thunder wings smite the water, heading
off chirp predators.
      Oftentimes I heard stumble

break flagging colour, I have noticed
      buddleia cornets
nod at the approaches of butterflies.

Advanced Driving

Slant glow shall recommend
the orthodox roads, help
them bloom, canalise their veins

in a veneer surface, collapsing
the veins so we can trace
but not travel. Esmée,

how are you doing? The last
I heard you had to carry
coat your bower. Rosamund,

your nets fell in a heap,
entangling the legs of sparrows—
if only they'd had claws

grapple would have slain them.
As it is, they billow
after you in free schools

prattling & diverse. Kip,
what happened to your wheels?
Sam—that wasn't so good

was it. Flooring creaks & pitch
starts flowing. Channels
clear, the gutters gather

minimal moss, garages void
open, cool trucks
nudge at loading bays, the lot

assembles birds. *Phal. Octavia*
overhangs in slim lamps;
a cloakroom discovers

morning on the tab—plenty
knock but do they
follow through, it's this coat

you left here, Donna.
Starch holds my tongue
off joining, still, down the road

polished deeps respond.
Colonial mahogany.
Perished rubber, brittle netting.

Fires spill out at first hand,
the burning wells
castle the otherwise flat corn,

birds plummeting in squadrons,
quiet slaughter
fuelling early air: there were

to have been deliveries
outsmart their fleeing shadows.
Loads tailgating.

Organise, Move and Back Up

Lines chair-lift their clutch of deep forest insects,
expropriating drops from humid air. Panoptic
creatures judged by a rangefinder, target cells
digitised in a block soup, draw down that fine-
beaded curtain, the curative darts, a lost tongue,
showing: *Only The Strong Survive, City of Ghosts.*
Now showing: the losses: gathered, irremediable.

Speculators float their up-country vision, piece
of action, ideal canopy-height perspective. Now
all earth's flocculence lies approved by yield,
sheaves pacify North Eastern hunting grounds.
The barbs of the ocean are drawn & justified,
insupportably dying in air. Steve, dinner. Friday,
switch cell account. Return DVD. Distinguish

Micronesian from Benin, peaceable tribes from
eaters of their fearless
            entrepreneurs of the new layer
sponsoring forest arts:
slit gong, eye slit, slit of the vulva, slit costume
            list & silt:

This potent object, this ritual object, this object
of unknown use,
            this slit object/
gash in a chilly envelope, gashes in a banner,
crucified body/
            into the midst of overplus
the ultimate floor-mix
            the multitudinous supper/
disclosure tears them apart, a disclosure troubles.

Blown out of the water. Depth-charge the dams.
The heavyweight tubers
jump up on the table,
        a load of opportunity
saturates the soil, saturates air, saturates water,
water to a breath-humid *fish-death! fish-death!*
        Boneless cemetery.

Glassy buoys jostle dead shoals, scant comfort
gapes for more. Scant cuts ease the opulent eye.
The eye coasts round the derrotero
        slitting parchment
                slitting vibrant blue.
Expectation gets one. The pageant hails one.
Available right now. An orchid, a monocarp/
forever & a day it blows.
Monotropa. Pale touch-me-not. The impatient.
Ghost flower. This is the last breeding pair.

Plied with birch bark & corn silk, infiltrators
might scrape by. Ghost kayakers had filched
yams, roasted them onshore, each spitting out
the tough bits, *Dogville, Mystic River.* Photo-op
gaze. Laugh off the alligator, grab a ragdoll,
profess to the okapi spirit, produce the phone.
The loss said soon mendacious, closes this slit

        listing, silted down.

Holidays in the Sun

for Laura Elrick

Each eager neck stretching, bug-eye prospecting
Pan-Pacific, Transworld, pigeon-like shrinks/
collars custom-built
      Then a cappuccino
breach ruffles smooth demeanour,
just a little this-way Have at you Alyssa, lance
the boil squinted plump
      on Newark's crumpled runway east,
glows, revolves, retinued with a scattering
semi-fledged have bristled redline then withdraw
into the cowling.
            Gobble up.

Each futile putsch, each promo Chickened out,
fearing deep lines, wowee, leaves Michael, Juan,
the finish lamper too high-mounted/
      fingerprints,
      iris prints
in the slurry sorted up-river, sorted Rikers.
Normal skin has become costume
en brochette which ordinarily
would break final straws/
now not wholly
      pinches off, & the muscle does the job,
shoving them back in the box into the silo They
have the hump not surprisingly
again & again like waves petrified underground.

Son you presume to mess with my coffee?—
got to, got to, stick your neck out/ extra shot &
poppies crack the deadpan, but can't

make the live case seductive
      You, arrogantly
resigned to take your ruthless path
if cool if casually,
who 'forged ahead' by muffin
      down the grain
      according to the flow swirls inside a flask
set in motion listlessly Its lazy droplets cake/
      the lookout
looking vulnerable, ID flapping void, beckons
      from that height/
      to that height/
enhanced at some observatory—
dizzy dizzy dizzy had to miss, when I say 'down'
I mean fluff OK?

Peeking over a dip a scoop, navigator all thumbs
bracketing some health clinic/ topsy-
      Turbot or veal, what-have-you
           I have galangal says Pete/
           brigantine
   slice, spare
   parts for crap scanners/ lookout
trains & screws his courage
tight upon the altimeter, misses
any vestige & shall gain
      White Target.
      Needless candle.
      Pointless estimate.
From this high the ice terror appears a sheet,
from this high the blood spill like a red duster

sign of wildfire zone,
from this high the flags of their claims look like
birthday cake candles on the white.
                    Protozoa
                    Asteroids
bunch in numerous mirror sites
yet more heavily distorted,
            light like mirror cream/
successor corporations skim off, earth glows,
unofficials shrink back into individual cartons.

D & M's abutment spoils. R & L can't divorce.
Dympna shoves it back
        Joe says Kiran.
    Roosevelt car
halts the train of question marks sways above
a complete expressway. Fowl with shorn spurs
peek from hutches, jolting to their last jolt.
A choice of wood at Crate & Barrel,
chocolate smothers well,
            Sino-Peruvian
blood & chocolate.
            Chicken dumped in a trolley
sweats naked shining. Java coffee,
children sun-spangled,
SUVs, APVs dropping their children off,
            Dulara! Paulette!
Robed in chocolate, tobacco, car fumes —
cough it up. Cough up. Not
        that TB chokes the end consumer,
            fair returns

float upward to the removed ceiling, set aside
where dense darkness grounds a brilliant earth,
a stopover
a feast-day in a collar of freedom.

Spiegeleisen

Brisk paper scythed the stands of maize
mutually upright. Stems less upright

elsewhere strove to keep with each other,
carried on chewing, carried on flicking

tumultuous layers. Paper cut rhetoric,
saturated cobalt ready to heal, thought

calm, few of the makings of weather,
millpool-flat, for all of its wide middle

void of reflection, crossing the period,
felled those stems of maize unsupported.

Daunted each ignored each one's need,
facing the same sickle, jeered their fall,

poor fist broken, rank smoothed over,
massing elsewhere, mass in a trace-cup

storing what traces convey or eradicate,
precious few might stem. Interpolation

rounded up: barbs, backchat, sneering,
arraigned with cries the hard harvest,

seed droplets swelled, a foolscap front
swept with cloud-blots. Now run over.

†

Across the blameless pavement writes
uncreased attention. Baby hypothetical

crawls sideways, soon to be adolescent
onto the market floor in Taipei, truly

stands & delivers. Brazenly she signals:
Hand raised, hand flexed for a flicker,

hand drops. Anachronistic blossom
thrives, who cared when her biography

summed up in one session, blue as it
skimmed & skirted, hosed down rivals,

dragged the lit air after her call. Finale,
a full sweep of ripe sheaves, silver cobs:

Stem.

Let rip.

Sway.

Rank these sowers of disorderliness,
vacuum cleaners trundle over the shore.
Elsewhere, burning glass

shakes out its ripples beautifully.
                              Membrane covers,
buttons & brutal rips-not-cuts. Presses/
a flattening blow/
until in shutting for the day, shutting
        Voluble, spring onto the floor

texters chirp & cellphones cap the offer,
desert jets,
a parched colonnade jets—
        The rubble rises in its fountains.

Occludes.

Music travels across the vacant middle.

View From the Air

Syllabled elegance makes a goose of itself
on purpose, so it appears at table
crowned in still-bright but obsolete
circuit boards:
      an ill-fitting
      vocal swirls
      out of punctuated
belches & compressed farts:
must implementation lie subordinate so
to fateful bands, the level-best of the
platform game, motive, liturgy or blockages?

The real geese, Canada geese,
compositely bob,
swim between cold strata,

waddle clumsily onto the bank, onto the low
loader, on the table.
Ready for table. Some other bird perhaps.
Their ductwork
stretches unto the first supplier.
It follows shame, follows self-despising,
assists at light irony.
It follows application,
sardonic but ever more distressed,
a blast-front
blowing evidence back on the table.

      Soft, soft, soft.
      A head like cotton wool
      picks up delicate fragments,

one scratch hooks attention, pinprick leak,
pinpoint rankness
irreproducible—*autre temps, autre mœurs,*
a dark dream of truth
shows where the scratches are,
scratches gathered into a skein
the wrong colour, the wrong declension,
all messed up,
reveals where the breaches jet.
Difference is so fast & dazzle-thatched
white feathers,
white feathers beating up a storm,

settled devise a cover for the second-guessing
shearing to encompass.

Less seamlessness.
More of the same.
Like new.

Taking Flight

Tenderly their rapture releases drones.
A wing & a prayer amplify
a thousandfold their single thought,
feathering across false hiddennesses,

imparting balked mercy. The very act
or path of separation complies,
forest-linked against the index, as
though to turn aside, turned a screw

so tightly as to stop a humane flow,
neutrally signing off the thread's
play & lock, certifying each package.
Whose packages come home to feast?

– a courtship this defiance perfects;
cross-threads tangle, bodies exchange,
secret viruses once sold in love
become the billets asked back urgently,

rapture finds its fulfilment in rape,
rape calculates its future in rapture.
Shall wingless drones reinstate
a corporate earth, shocked-still waters.

Steam Cuisine

Out there parades overt,
           the pan hi-tails long enough
accessible, enacted, on demand
           consanguineous & worldly.

Out there stays the hand,
           music notable by its absences
rates what follows, slips narrative
           teetering about the flies

back into its *mise en scène*:
           the bay flushes violent red,
weeds choke propellers of little
           boats whose catch displays

fantastic ceilings, spiral
           housing, mutant gastropods/
           what plug
stays internal, rates authentic or
           conditionally xenomorphic?
           Internal
piping had been thought-over, wire-
           framed, tomatofish/
           stabilized by guy-
ropes as a theatre
capsule you distract from but a shrug
           won't do it, capsule
like a tree house pinioned by a nigh
-on full-on line of inquiry.
           That tastes.

Insinuates.
Totals up. Takes away abruptly.
Suffers the slot children.

Turning turtle they might live
        violently. The transgeneae
slip between stretchmarks, breed
        where blur allows

developments, white organic
        tenderloin, task-centred
statutes define fish but stomp
        Alice's parsley: their rugged

tares shall be reaped, her gift
        plump sheaves, a stem cell
sequence turneth all to hump
        the driven herd, Io,

Io brought to birth by the herdsman,
        cultured overhead in cloud.
Alice occupies her trench, dirt
        clouts her fingers:

        Mutant clubhouse active
dead looking at their own nails
tapering, then touch the grease nipple
tip-fingered but no fingerprints
identify a newcomer
        lost from his branch/

Hold, hold/
through sandwich
          poised displacement/
courtesy the Nile or Great Zimbabwe/
rooting for the autogene on autopilot.
Did you just *emerge*?
Where's he descended with his creel?
      Phospholipid this:

Sill-face caper.

Candle-hip kiss-toe.

Glyphosate bound.

The trait for adaptability
pegged for a point of susceptibility.
          Pain replicant says.
                  Some slippage says.
The imitation of life restages life at
level best afflicts an invisible hand
with tendonitis.
Propellers cough, twine
          cordage swings, little bodies
bouncy in their safety nets
          wrapped over, wrapped over,
                  pan-thalassic
                  wine-dark

wrapped telomeres. A bloody nail
　　scores like the exotic
penetrates its microwaveable pack,
　　births itself in steam,

that the induced mutant rips open,
　　said marker bound
to its own breath, brooch
　　pinned in mink-like fur,

growls at the front of house,
　　red in the face, catastrophe!
dog-leg collapse, a curled inoperativeness
　　borne out on a tray, a parabolic

turnaround for a bow. Applaud this understudy.
　　Crocodilian mouse.
Mice. Observe after breach-birth
　　flurries of notes speed upwards.

In Camera

A pair of black swans entering below the line,
props the single-digit lake as an attraction.

A pair of black swans entering below the line,
props the single-digit lake as an attraction.

Designate it as a prop. A rent in the mirror
sheet took over schedules, a black cicatrice.

Designate it as a prop. A rent in the mirror
sheet took over schedules, a black cicatrice—

portrayed to the life in its white suppuration.

†

The swan of sapping scores, that's the other
75 to figure out the solitary into its figure.

The swan of sapping scores, that's the other
75 to figure out the solitary into its figure.

Swarm that is, flock, like sucking out of a
glass river, flights left drifting, brittle bones.

Swarm that is, flock, like sucking out of a
glass river, flights left drifting, brittle bones—

shadowed by the clammy, metropolitan day.

†

Or if picking off the flanks with suffixes, fit
sharp-shoot gallowglasses fire that postulate
the swans trained upon them, made their sort
plume never condescends. The black plume

dips below the surface, black foam rimples
a flopping-over seam, black earth is ploughed
waveringly, table elements & fish scales
gush from a polyp they agglomerate towards.

†

No scruples when the wadding jerks away,
leaving sponged lines abutting against dawn.

No scruples when the wadding jerks away,
leaving sponged lines abutting against dawn.

Bare-faced shadows were the heated response
glowing had conveyed intimately stretched.

Bare-faced shadows were the heated response
glowing had conveyed intimately stretched—

swan cuneiform pressed on white caulking.

Elementary Film

after Abban Kiarostami

So to test the water. Folded-wing hippogriffs
crowd the paved shadows, they'll be realised

lake from rill to shingle to humpback bridge
to this world, whose cinematic stiff, jewelled

assembly, scurrying through light, summoned,
signs undismayed. The courtesan's shadow

scuds & dragonflies, dragonflies float. Rain
clouds rub, overlapping overlapping, steered

confident when she glides to rendezvous, she
sings the while. It's raining, wakes nervous

hippogriffs who pawing the bridge in theory,
send their representatives, solid-hoofed

to break apart shadows, vein in spider glaze
lake from rill to shingle to humpback bridge,

veins of light lift a dragonfly. Light-trimmed
her stiff, jewelled ruffles had been fingered

& thought soft: the world keeps a distance,
disappointed, this world says so little, slough

a little inflates, furls its several consequences
into the hideyholes, bright pockets stitched

to a landscape clearly planted in all senses.
These are odd creases, much as I'd thought,

says she, it's chance the wrinkles of avoiding
should like this repeat the wrinkles of meeting.
        Chance indeed:

                Best thing were
lurch stunned on their glittering footplates,
shining bridge cables
        stunned here to drift
without response or proposition, turn ugly
witnessing a street assault, a transferred
        package, angry at un-
        reasonable distress,
where the fired body remains intact yet still
unknowably damaged,
                or if known unfelt:

Best thing to pad through shattering puddles,
        safe in a carbonised
        wire tunnel, anti-
vandal paint, flash bounces back from a hurt,
makes glass opaque,
        wing-backed hippogriffs
fly off to Ireland, Nubia or Cyprus
                bearing others' markings:

once these furlings have unfurled, rolled back
shadows superimposed to show a causeway

creep like eventide beckons, lays on thick
lake from rill to shingle to humpback bridge,

horses of instruction are recalled to the stables,
leaving the field to monsters. Light delegates

fleet of foot, the outriders to flies' agitation,
tangle with black candlewick, intrusive twigs,

imperative softening. These serried courtesans
break towards their summoners, they flutter

not so much skin-deep as a translucent body
showing its inner shadows' assembly. Rented

pockets alive, every grab-bag seething. None
says she, I'd be content to loiter, deep scale. I

see my convolutions layer, a slapped surface
                coinage/
        light skint/
what do I have to do
        with such invitation
soon clears up. She's shouldering her satchel,

forward feet, shadows snatching at her fiercely,
lake from rill to shingle to humpback bridge.

Road Kill

Ice was looking a pool, or
the wet road the bird
crashes into, a river

was looking a road of ice
harrowed regularly
like a freezing TV set,

& it does look so.
Vertically in their piling-up
black fur, above—

Ambitiously in that bridge
closed to foot
traffic & bicycles—

ice cuts, ice coaxes,
fans out their silvery backs'
leachate. Select one.

It has a deathly look. Scroll
figures in their blurred
revealing sort—

Select a second.
A flock seeks to purify
itself with its own dazzle,

shucking off the outriders,
peeling its penumbra
so to cover all—

look ice despicably would
misdirect, better
tread naked earth

than fledge the road-
metal, overglaze
with an opaque, pure look

the drifting channels. Pay
heed. Beset by 100Mz care.
Too well-matched

they're cross-dressing,
huntresses or decoys. As on
ice the stria drag,

some pretend to wings,
a snowy egret is straggling
over ice furrows.

Karelian Birches

Thick green said its
      oxyacetylene brochure—
fit the best—
these show its crocuses, these
hardened off
shrank. Circular saws
blunted light on hard earth,
patinated, brown
gaps between sessions,
      mend those
with sky-blue piping,
bend leaden sky around light.

    †

Berries overstock the thorn,
dragging boughs with
      old plenty.
Their point here was 'looks'
into a full term.
Thorn squeezes soil
as at the first, the single
thorn
twists over the single prairie,
squeezing it for water.
      No further sessions—
sky-blue unvaryingly.
The urns. A scented snuff.
A Karelian snuff-box.

†

Feel the pinch.
Stintless
locusts cedaring the skies.
Unceasing birches
wavered, tensed together
    face to face
stitching teeth.
Lines of mastic had assisted.
By when, green backcloth
had engulfed
    contractors' cabins,
creasing the acropolis,
cantilevered blocks of blood.

†

There is a low cloud.
The sound box
perches
sudden flowering.

†

An incident, granted,
gathered at its corners,
chopped off where corners
    held to surpass,
germinating fleas
germinating ants,
beyond would go multiply
smoke in ramparts,

the tundra
knows no basement,
      Western Mountains
know no caves,
      so their hash of
rotten marble
brochures amassing,
dropped from blue clouds—
obvious letterhead:

Say the dishes dry,
say a stove-corroded pan
      gathered cloud
out in the open,
tethering shallow depth,
a hundred thousand berries,
maybe two
days of flower to go.

      †

A thin brown stain, armed.

Marram Riff

No other place than this
kind of meant.
Thus it means. Thus. As though a spring-
board sprang into may,
as though a harness for the will
struck of its own volition,
no other place could be expected
as it were, as it went,
no other place could be as is,
reprieved through hard-wiring, saved
not religiously, grappled
not timetabled, even so a spongy bed
soaks up then releases
then rebounds.
Snippy cradles, trembling sofas ask more.
Yellow
parallels, but feels wrong,
green feigning succour,
blue pre-emptive tags rustle. Not a thing.
All this
mock assembly urges forward,
cover-up does too,
scheduled trains run at times
both directions down the stretch
expansive, sprung on ballast, overwrought
sightseers
head straight home, or would have
had they motive enough,
but caught on promontories,
desultory
puffs of smoke waste their impetus
across a miniature layout,

map of the first industrial era.
              Oh yes?
No-one left the railhead.
Bring a voided cheque to the till.
Polish a fine fowling-piece. 1.4M gap,
celestial opportunity.
           What did they
imagine? But this
place they leave, they leave to find great,
delivering their tin & whisky songs,
elastic turf.
           Prevalent stalks.
Rivers slow with chalk waste
soothe an Inspector of Mines's throat,
           imitators
smarmily throng,
fight for his breathy testament,
            his imitators
pitch their yarns of wayfaring,
let down, much too late,
tussle for best places, sharpen knives . . .
           That's close, where they
should have expected to find the surface,
            spring-loaded shells.

Marram Grass

The xerophiles
break down mouths of agitated burrows,
straggle over pine barrens,
                              tongues
loll in a shore-long slurping line-up,
like roughening, like fade,
like smouldering if said of water or like
fluctuating said of opals. Like
filthy mouth, beneath her breath
mutters.
                Combustible
atop a glassed-in wave.
                        Comprehensive
multicolour upload, outputting via red.

Like assertive
        quadbikes & SUVs have carved
salty ducts, power
ribs shuddering to break loose, diesel
trails burn the water
        Shifting of hunched sand
won't deter the xerophiles, self-healing
ramparts were OKed,
        like paths adjust,
voices on the shore drift outward,
        then if scudding home,
speak this margin to a line drawn ragged
further up—
weed or pebbles, buoyant blocks—
blocks carved, blocks erode

into these naiads,
porn stars. The xerophiles trudge past.

Xerophiles throng onto their club floor,
a teeming underthatch,
     soak the wodge of thickener
voluptuous with veins,
             dead sheet, wrinkled verge
sucking at their slow heels,
water strops a salt ledge,
     dogged, automatic, licking
out some lodging place, a lick erosion
         spiriting the sand,
as though pile-up
were a highway's purpose, watch-making
were a whale's, or if a junk oil,
actually it claims here its true flame
stinks & gutters sootily . . .
     look actually the thing was
         the thing was
    saprophyte, delicately lipped
Pan away,
down the coast a new lagoon's cedilla,
isn't
     there the place to gather,
there where stinging whispers clench—
     what else would pine
pickets lodge into,
     plain as day,
     bunch in breathing columns,

converse
like ill wind was said of dust-devils or like
cinematic, said of summer snow.
        Aggrieved & isolated,
stuck on his promontory
a lookout kicks an engine & rips a ditch,

        the xerophiles'
lips sealed & lids gunged with weeping,
routinely like myelinic sheaths
absorb light's shocks,
reels & cassettes banked against erosion,
        will they mourn prospectively
the micro-habitat in mind, the one
place they ever visit.
Back they stumble
                xerophiles
dolloped over sand on walkways
concreted with bonds & hot
municipals, their roots
        reputedly provisional, or like
rippling if said of sand wispily or mainly
piled high if said of water.

Marram Mat

Heat intensifies & the parasols
mushroom brightly alongside the lagoon,
     buttoning lips, unlidding,
a gentle swooshing draws flotillas
confident of their wish to drift.

Nobody's home stood, another
     well-intentioned, moated it &
salivate despite, & get a load of
humanly automatically
     was that meant? was that where

what will have been had been suborned
by nuisance tweezers
     unbuttoning lips, lidding
over what just filters down
anxious at the compulsion to drift

from the crown of the head to the
tip of the chin,
     from the palm to the temple
underpinning—& such a buzz of
competent perversity circled the lagoon,

     heat intensified & parasols
like casts one single reflex threw, tensed
above the elastic inlet,
feathering each shadow, eyed
salaciously, but no girl promenades,

what were bodies trail off,
the loose prow veers as though to drift:
 a white-bangled hut,
a salty kiss, a devious
meander to the ticket machine,

pointless, faded as the mouth's foil split
through chalk-foamy wash,
 hunting dogs had faltered,
infant grey lions were snoozing
upon a victory pedestal,

 white-bready bulbs, disengage
when a detachment touched
 beastly deliberately,
protozoic hubbub in the drowned world
summarily silenced,

squished, shoved off thick pontoons,
whose overlapping bites, half-wolf half-
 dog rips into their throats,
these ageing
heads of the town widowed

drift expressionless but steered
involuntarily through indent or dimple,
dearly missed voice,
 inner air fleshed out
amidst the welter, airy pocket

ocean trembles to reproduce,
its salty ploughshare pushes. Shrouded
face congruity & compass
frees itself down foam rails,
       dispersed imagined unified,

long tresses rearrange features

a fading day's heat plucks & contracts.

Marram Creep

for Allen Fisher

That's the place no trace of a doubt.
Grass pokes its files through tract matting,
waste ground at Homerton/
      at Hackney Wick
flourishing yellow slippers, silvery cans,
      rough
lines draw Gorran Haven, superimposed
as when an unlit walkway lurched
across the strip, red stars,
ill-tethered buoys rejigged to some
sort of semblance:
      Plaistow,
      Portland Bill,
the tidal flags warped & fluttered,
signalling their unison could see traduced
the one who saw,
beckoning furiously behind his eyes
to freeze such arrant show,
its littered letters, titles, front of house
      tuned inferentially, a dry run
with recycled plastics:
      View at risk. Fly-
tipped electric stoves, fridges rust,
      driers carry forward, losses
grew advantageous, rigging whistled
positively, lotteries of
loss arterial
through steel rocks whose lizard hinter-
land went packing,
rock & concrete chunks, discarded
forms, these rubbished over
Worm's Head & Mile End Park,

                    cut off by mid-afternoon,
capitulate, self-effacing.
Convoys scoot around, collide
against what will have been, their choral
up-beat narrative on sand
belts punts on future highs,
                    the asphalted
corollary, avid fans
suspended by their latterday from railings
edging skyways, highways, water tanks,
runways of rapture, reinforced
          front doors, like
          window hatch, like
former conductivity, heaven's gate
smacked by kicking kids, a tinny carcass
clattering at pebbles flung,
tin underbelly—
made for perspicacity—
                    entices
up against it, thick striated glass sheets:
watch at a safe distance:
          Here had ocean swole,
here the sky, monstrous both
with their aspiring depths & heights,
deliberately inflamed
behind sleep-motorised shutters
          Singular pornography
cast its slides
across the mank underloft, staining
cobalt mowers cropping grassy files like
violet rivets rainbows,
what transition,

come to that,
trailed its cross on barrows over a foreland
sadly scissored,
dropped its cardboard
clutter on the faded spit acquired,
though its mock-up left unblemished,
gyroscope in his forehead
fo'c'sle swung about,
certified what fossilised in wing cases,
deviants
espousing a self-righting model,
knocked together quickly
gunmetal finish/
however kludged,
spoke, harassed & tugged sleeves' manifest
candy bar reissue in turquoise.
The visualisers ask: What will have been?
What will the big deal back then be
Like envision?
like see here? If only.
OK cully.
The fat of the land sucks & the bones jar.
Supernumerary waves fan across.

Marram Scaffold

Following Barbara Guest

Climb the sand horn, the aspirated engine does.
Salts darken in the day's advance.

What unearthly reeled back
designed to withstand, with its big warm opulence

attracted swimmers. Hence the cove
colour pencil. A choir diminishes in wavelets

floppy garlands paddle. The wash is what piles up
against a construction site,

swept that mudbank clear as mud,
dissonant for fear of dissonance. Trembling air dies

or does the one stood at once transformative.
You must undergo. As does fragile,

as dies the pinafore as gaping flies,
instances I'd weathered & whose molten ordnance

jumped but without aspiring, but then jump
might no more than drop. Darkening lights,

a sickle falls & visible monuments
stand up to their knees, prurient groping, a wrong

headed scrabble under the revealed lid,
measures dunes refaced for masquerade, like the

bolted heads below the cube, an engineer
mouth taped in the shadow of a smashed aqueduct.

Believe sand. Convince sand.
The absorbed woman takes down the curtain,

twilight presses on these deserts she has cornered.

Marram Clutch

The cheeping throstle attaches itself, cries of
infants blade her face, clots mulberry-
stain covers. Many have details
off pat: as so lightly tacky,
tiny weights depress the fretwork
jalousie, screen behind which all wiped
to order, dominoes, bones ranked by function,
smiles cast afloat—an assistant
helps her to the most viable:
these were designed to last over the ridge,
to value, spare from the set values, ride
on the face of them,
for if too achingly lovely they'd leech;
better trade up than suffer their pug iniquity,
death-in-life beguiled, blackbird-fringed.

If quick, in a cat's evasion soul can be glimpsed,
& in the reflex heart of the parent,
soul leaps. Salvation by deeds
drives revolutionary cadre, cherished
in low huts, its flowers haunt the historied.
Trigger response shakes the canopy,
flares to moral effect. Chewing it over,
stuffing the arc with paper, so you obstruct
the only device of integrity competent.
You couldn't make up, reclaiming land
in a polder, key the blocks & cement them,
learning love for the waves:
balance fails, the tentative work crashes.
Familiars, over-familiar
wait for a flame, purring, counting on love.

How the sand-bank ramps for the wall!
How the surf staggers a bulldozing
share of ocean, surely though each has a cellular
implant—not so fast, my
souling owns no inner compunction,
trenching, banking, coaxing the wind-blown,
shoring the tide-torn, much like
one launched
live from a sea wall, smack! thoughtless,
burst through a drum-skin, saving a drowner,
clenched would lift, as hearing stars
would have conditioned to jump...
don't even think of it: bracing at barriers,
bystanders rush the bridge,
sweep a knock-kneed hero to face his hero,

his breath escaping in steamy bursts. Outfalls
drench those less than agile
under their reflux. Out amid sea traffic,
choke mid-gasp, then muster at the diastole
beneath cliffs, swirl about their base;
deeper breath responds, its vestiges
damp down the fluttering of beautiful souls.
Though mulberry stain spreads,
imbues regret for autumn's frolic
groves of plucking, squeezing, even
heedless tugs of fruit—resolve will quicken
each to his own, reunite
the stand-up with his straight man,
diver with his dealer. Their arbitrageur
inflicts a staunch, a stalwart

flocks the gulls, one waveform, one standstill
complicates hotly, breath retorts, breath
smocks with blossom, fires the
earth's exaltation, wire-fizzing murk
pumps through skeletal chicks;
a murrain rush, a spate of breath
decomposing fleshy files, such a cruel
riposte sweeps off flecks of
cockle pickers, picks off sky-walking scaffolders,
crushing rocks & trees into a mortal exigence.
Mud bubbles in its clear capsule,
that activity
far pumps support, & if they sputter
thousands die. Come soothe this ear.
Shall the life's chamber thrill with sweet song?

Sound counsel breeds a retinue, whatever sings.
These were paths, these were grooves
more like it: ivy climbed in charts,
linnets pulled taut wires beyond
what ear could verify, perusing openness
for a value. Vacant animal
prised out of the mould in misch metal,
yours to occupy
with low deposit: defiantly wasn't impressed,
more intervals! she murmurs from her
follied cot, catching eyes as they passed,
keeping her marbles. More gaps!
inside outward-crooking arms. Yes love incurs
heath heuristics, in hell's teeth
authoritative chambers grew loved & mossy—
plugged must thwart stimuli—:

but reflex housebreakers kick in their seals,
sharp loss plucks by this by this,
such panache! no history but atmosphere but
dispossession, slows & clogs the
whetstone wings of splayed-out swans,
swoop over their event scene.
Roles reverse, stripped-down aggressors
roam rubble,
dive in glistening ditches, glare
off aluminium frames. They compensate
oppressively, in unsought presence.
When I saw you scoured & screened,
brightly flickering, smile re-set,
I saw myself applied like an icon's resin layer,
but now like many haunt these cavities,

wire mesh filled with droplets, horizontal drift,
skyline, landfall, mist, low cloud:
a mud-slide sometimes jolts
pent files of traffic, white commission,
milling stars with noise to fritter.
What if giving thought should interfere,
tending lines firm — no, not to fear:
breath, motive sediment, clear
the river mouth: while on a colonial shore,
laden currents bank on the future,
men smack bones, girls wear brakes of
coral, nor it seems impossible
for life to soil the features, smiles touch
an image mulberry-stained
slumps over the bed-rail & lets slip her cup.

Marram Edging

A carnival of rhomboid truth unrolls—
arrayed below the cork & iron,
the hydrogen & shoreline gunk—
mind clenches, love grasps,
        gods seize their moment,
asteroids intervene in huge flat channels,
arranged incongruity.
        Eat fast but hold the
        pit until it calcifies

in one throat, one ordeal
one tested & tried
        triumphant wick,
between the busy fox of meteorology
& altars of depleted head-cheese,
fraying soft stock, drop a line.
The sinuses are labelled Wa'habi—
        logical positivism—
                carnal fire—

dredge up sand on tar on lead
on old rope on money. Carnal fire,
        pre-emptive breath,
choke that flushes alabaster,
substitute warmth. Well what if
evening shines like a white flank
refusing entry or any acknowledgement,
& all the queuing
tie again the bold block

venting secretly from three-star lockers,
promises still fresh
     like milky drugs,
     those notaries
dignified round a frigid lozenge,
studying its form,
what they put in they get/ plus
     accompanying book,
exact same turf, same distance:

get up off those haunches,
what shall have been below
seeps from a slow front-loading slot,
     what no bar-code!
     stickily decompensates.
The subjunctive
quilt of thought,
shapely foam
pads out along the sine-wave, modifies,

dunes thought full of feather ticking

rubber billfold perishing & spoiling

modern grid still centring each cipher

He is upright now on a trolley, head lolls.

Marram Nursery

a

I know I knew I knew I knew
all over the iconic cupboard,
          flat as arseholes. So this season
reaches after danger & laughter,
fruit bottled on the bough,
bunches of thin shoots rise on thin soil
          exactly as depicted,
each assumes its stance of live-&-let—
                    one manic zeal
                    one bug-eyed,
one through whose sweet enforcement
earth deodorises & it bears
spangles, Mars, Skittles, Wotsits,
          Big Mac boxes/
cyan harvest,
          some shall have ruffled feathers,
          you're shitting me,
          not if I could help it didn't
          strip mall. Who gives a toss—
others thrive timely,
but fermenting in their buds
played with like heat-sealed packets
          colostomy disposal.
Don't positions remedy this glut?
          Wouldn't you know
          a steaming pile
snap-frozen
levers up the low limbs, black-gartered
metal boughs
where someone of my name prowls

        between aluminium tags,
something like a net
loss
raises opal shoots, brightly packaged
icons, novelty items
crinkle wide,
                singed prayer flags
                cancelled fingers
flaunt redeemable clippings,
        chip or bar or stick
lost into the pram void,
last light breaks in water, heads detach.

b

Yellow waxy pouches, diligent spikes
clamour to safeguard
              the pastille dropping
wrapped in small print.
              In general
              as a syntactical rule
leaked creams slather burnt lower limbs,
I know I knew I know I knew,
ribs or tips
restored by Egyptologists, perk
mass in pseudo-sap, pulp
prickly pear,
              aloe vera smeared onto
the wreath'd trellis of a working brain
              flew their stall or pew
              incandescent, mad to wilt
flitted in high grass.
Shed keys scattered twirled showered
funerary confetti,
petals fell like smuts,
              what's insolently
raised up shall be cut down to size,
all hands lost
              layer of hardcore, sheath,
baked topsoil, one who bore my name
forced through the narrows, hush
stilted progeny coil in tensile knots,
              limping into loud wind,
              smothering eye catches,
              smoking out

attention swarm
                    not one irreplaceable,
pocking new-laid asphalt, infests
the slack mind of the groomed gardener,
surfaces a cesspit with hyphens.
          Then shall the float rise
as snow & smoke thicken Indiana.
The visible is loss's signature,
but the lost exult: This is freedom
plain as a pikestaff
          (whatever pike denotes)
a kind of float with chopped head on top
starts bouncing, soon to plunge.

Marram Chorus

Look who throng the daylight overhangs
    Look how old school
party scenes can't be erased,
tangle in their heads,
        while of all licks the stalest
keep them on the button,
check they self-impersonate
through wave on wave.
        Lubricated sirens
joust in muted verbals, but this one . . .
    no restraint
            like her
dirty writhe would make her a rebuttal
to all meanness, even the eventual
to a straggly henceforward,
    breaks meaning dawns.

        Look how opalescence
foam-laces
daintily where tongue-nymphs recite:
Meet Kirsty. Meet Alicia.
        Haunches of stinging sand
shift under rooted webs, zephyrs
whipping up gold, nymphs
sight-reading seedhead ripple,
        seedhead ripple
tracing ocean shrugs,
      scallop
sherbet popping underfoot,
      she's wrong-footed, right
foot forward, fizzing reflexes,
groynes collapse, dunes huddle,

sand must, it
has to, pass for a fair setting
    This side of darkness's usurping.
Layers shift across layers.

Look what sand warps,
like just schmoozing with this inlet,
        wheedles on the off-chance,
languidly slowly stretched:
    Palæmon, arbiter of epithets,
keeps his weather eye, his beady
fixed on silt-supporting water,
    rasping, re-gilding,
knocks the barnacles away,
    dredging harbour roads,
entices each its tutelary,
prodding her to flaunt, dervishing
along a modular judgmental wharf—
The xerophiles disparaging her beauty,
snarl . . .
like really such a fake pulls,
like the affected bleed, o pull another
frozen gold,
their fallen faces strapped in place,
    lazy eyes.

How glorious to persist in error!
What gleaming flats!
Look, visible exceptions
ply the oars,
    her hair streams
nonpareils, hundreds & thousands spin,

Delphic flapping
of attendant birds, heads of sea-serpents —
first by background, by series, by set,
stripped of their setting,
tremble in new imminence:
      pink flossy
pelmet swollen over light's long drop
swashes with her boat's shipping water,
      like her
objects cusping to & fro,
eyes on her wake
she scans for her pursuer, so she pulls
into a calm front
      gradually capsized,
referring to the sun of course.

Marram Trench

The face of flesh I think quickens,
entablature of what plays
through ring-bound hands. Probably has.
    Some returning flutter,
some festooned
with rubber lengths
    smooth down. Grass kowtows,
cowed by their workmanship,
springs back behind their
tense ruts.
A red button blips above the exit door.
    As though a warning-off
reliably entices. It does. Most often.

The face of flesh, understand,
follows after what shall have followed—
    see they return,
the swift to scratch, swift to expose.
Elbows stuck out from a coverlet
sayings poke through, rib
the sandboy excruciated in his grass skirt,
a triple thickness of
artificial skin had been dispensed
in liquid form, from sappy eyes—
    so this pupa
bound with sticky tape weeps
what would soon count as experience:
    It dies. It dies.

We have lift-off. Now purfle with
fat zeros, naked light-bulbs,
now rig the mic for a mime's dance,
set padded chairs;
        across the deathly amphitheatre
skin shrinks
to its perfected role, straps
encircle head dummies,
snag the windows, glitch the latches:
        save the day, try not
obstructing recessed lights from
running through the day's more concrete,

flattening the outside, rappelling all faces
like screen doors relocate birches
otherwise messy, otherwise scratch.
        Miniature positions
stitched in these outfits in the
nick of time stretching to accommodate
vault or caracole,
        jumped from a standing start,
merged into the press, itched to
test their magazine, tease open
a deracinated tight-wad,
        spread on grass
with whispered premonition. Yes
fatty marrow adds a sim-card
giveaway, banquets on its own resources.

The face of flesh, puffy, water-logged,
a single seed lodged in one sinus,
senses eyes exude, no, weep
spontaneously, that's more general
to the system,
                    its progress-chaser
swelling blood parties, also
proved compelling, eggshell blue
pegged tight
in a demonstration
of what little consequence it had
to profess, once setting was discounted—
                    it was, it was,
but there can be no pure negative.

The face of flesh suffers,
but what follows? Hives in their growth
stock the testbed,
each hollow has its crystal pellet
light plays over like extrapolating,
like zigzag.
                    The crystal stent
collects more rays which puncture
buttery richness.
            Evidently the house
wanted drainage, until surface
run-off from the glazed sand
rilled the path through
cockle beds, to encompassing trenches.

Printed in the United Kingdom
by Lightning Source UK Ltd.
115336UKS00001B/298-324